Imitators of the Fly

Imitators of the Fly

A History

PETER HAYES

Tight-lines!

COCH-Y-BONDDU BOOKS
ANGLING MONOGRAPHS SERIES NO. 1
2016

IMITATORS OF THE FLY: A HISTORY
TWO HUNDRED AND FIFTY NUMBERED PAPERBOUND COPIES
PLUS TWENTY-SIX LETTERED HARDBOUND COPIES
HAVE BEEN PRODUCED IN THE
COCH-Y-BONDDU BOOKS ANGLING MONOGRAPHS SERIES

THIS COPY IS NUMBER .94.

Pictures on pages 6, 31, 32, 38, 42, 46, 49, 52, 53, 63, 80, 90, 91
by courtesy of the Flyfishers' Club, all rights reserved.

ISBN 978 1 904784 68 5

Coch-y-Bonddu Books Ltd
Machynlleth, Powys, SY20 8DG
01654 702837
www.anglebooks.com

Acknowledgements and thanks

This 'potted history' stands on the shoulders of giants, and could not have been produced without extensive involvement and research carried out by my colleagues as follows:

- David James has read all the proceedings of all the Flyfishers' Club main committee meetings since it was founded, and prepared précis summaries of all of them which I have found absolutely invaluable in helping to sort out what happened when, as well as giving insights into the personalities and politics of the club over time. David lent me the NFSC minute book and has been extremely supportive of our work on the natural fly collections: indeed I think their restoration was his idea in the first place.

- Our past Curator, John Morgan; our new Curator, John Knott; and David Beazley, our Librarian, have each done their damnedest to find the Great Tabulation – and may yet succeed!

- Tony Hayter in writing his definitive books on Halford and Skues, and in making his personal library, and his recall of salient facts and stories, unstintingly made available to my own researches; and Dr Andrew Herd's work in his many books on the history of the fly and flyfishing have made possible this brief overview of the history of imitation that would otherwise have stumbled to a halt.

- Dr Peter Barnard through his scholarship and scientific expertise, that again he has made available both to myself and to the Flyfishers' Club, has made possible a deeper and clearer understanding of what was going on, particularly with reference to Mosely: in addition to volunteering to reverse engineer the preservation techniques involved in the fluid collection and re-perfect them.

- Dr Cyril Bennett has been good enough to get involved in the restoration project right from the start, has volunteered to contribute his superb photography to a planned companion document in addition to capturing and breeding through the actual specimens that we require, and has turned his scientific knowledge to helping us get it all correct.

- Theo Pike has been kind enough to read this in his capacity as Editor of the *Flyfishers' Journal*, and his comments and editorial input are very much appreciated, as are those of Paul Schullery.

- The team's thanks are due to the Library and Collections Subcommittee; and to the General Committee of the Flyfishers' Club for their support of the restoration efforts, and of the interpretative and historical work involved.

- We have also been very appreciative of the help of the club's secretary Paul Varney, who has periodically leapt cheerfully from his busy desk to measure the dimensions of watch glasses, verify the presence or absence of the Harry Mears dedication plate, take useful photographs, and so on.

The Flyfishers' Club has provided me with every possible assistance in preparing this book. Indeed it could not have been written without the opportunity to study carefully the Club's wonderful collection of flyfishing memorabilia and artefacts. However it should be clearly understood that the content of this book is entirely my own and all statements, interpretations and conclusions reached are mine and in no way should be thought of as representing the beliefs of the Flyfishers' Club, its officers or members.

Peter Hayes
January 2016

Foreword

I wrote this for my own benefit initially, because I was getting confused. We current fly fishermen are living in a constantly developing and now rather sophisticated sport which is nonetheless constantly reinventing itself. We are engaged in a sport which has a living history behind us, an exciting developmental present, and a hopefully attractive future. I had become curious about the relationship between the past and the present, and I had become involved in exploring it: but it had started to confuse me. Out of respect for, and interest in our angling progenitors, I had been looking in detail at what we do now, and exploring how we got to do what we do now and how far back things go.

As the reader will know if they have spent any time looking at it, there are vast amounts of writing, vast numbers of facts – not to mention tens of thousands of fly patterns – and these are hard to assimilate in a meaningful way even when, as they have been, they are presented in appropriately comprehensive detail by the great angling historians of the present day. It is easy to get lost, and lose the storyline, and even forget who's who, and when each thing happened, in spite of being fascinated at every point in the journey through their books. So this small book started out as a kind of personal *Bluffer's Guide to the History of Flyfishing*. Then, the more detail I went into and the more revealing the extra facts and angles I uncovered, the more it grew, and the more I enjoyed adding viewpoints and illustrations to it.

In addition to the storylines and the personalities involved in developing the flyfisher's imitation of the fly, both technical and societal changes have been massively influential, and I've included reviews of these. Yet many of the things we do today have their origin in the distant past and in the inventive brains of perceptive anglers not a whit less intelligent than ourselves. Who would have thought, for example, that fishing a lead-weighted nymph on a short line with an indicator section in the leader, 'Czech style' would have been recommended by two flyfishing writers in the late 1600s? That the problem of selective trout would have been dealt with over two centuries ago? The bulk of this book however deals with the explosion of imitative and presentational progress that occurred between the mid-1800s and the mid-1900s, and I have tried to keep the whole thing short enough to be easily digestible. I make no apology for my having divided it up into short paragraphs with rather newspaper-headline-type headings: I did it for me, but I hope it helps you too, and makes the journey through this short book an easy and entertaining one.

Minute books of the Flyfishers' Club

Imitators of the Fly

The Melting Pot of Creativity and Development from
1800 to Living Memory, its Personalities and Storylines

During the period from the early 1800s up to living memory, flyfishing burst out of narrow banks with a flood of creativity and new ideas, partly driven by interest in science, partly driven by commercial opportunities, partly driven by flowering technologies, and crucially fed by burgeoning wealth and an emerging middle class. This short book looks at this period of accelerating development and at the personalities that drove it. The review takes us up to the post-World War II marker of the middle of the last century: my reason being that what came after 1950 is pretty much in living memory. A review of the post-war development of flyfishing up to the present day would take years, simply because of the enormous mass of brilliant work that has followed the period I have chosen. And within living memory readers will have their own experience and opinions, whereas within the period in review there is much that has not been common knowledge until now, and that I am setting out to reveal.

A slow and narrow stream for four preceding centuries

The course of flyfishing's progress from the 1400s, the time of the earliest extant English writings with the *Treatyse* circulating in manuscript before it was printed, through to the end of the 1700s, was beautiful, often poetic, aspirational and instructive, but constricted to a relatively narrow course out of which it seldom strayed in terms of

A stream uncorked and bursting out of narrow banks

development. The thinking and teaching of the leading personalities followed the work of those who had gone before, almost as in an oral tradition, even though it had become a written one. For example, the work of Izaak Walton which seemed so fresh and new, has now been shown to have owed a great deal to the prior work of William Samuel in *The Arte of Angling*, published in 1577 (and now surviving in only one copy, which may in fact have belonged to Walton himself).

So in terms of flyfishing development, new methods, new ideas, new flies and soforth, you could be pardoned for seeing the literature of those first four centuries as flowing down a narrow channel, not entirely without new ideas but without any great degree of inventiveness, and certainly without any great commercial development, until the start of the 1800s.

I have, in my book *Fly Fishing Outside the Box: Emerging Heresies* (Coch-y-Bonddu Books, 2013), pointed out with as much evidence as I think makes it un-arguable, that the early flyfisher was not fishing the wet fly as most people have thought, but was trying as hard as he could to accurately imitate the hatched fly on the surface of the water with one or more flies that he constructed as 'dryly' as he could, he himself as the angler being responsible for keeping them afloat, and in lifelike imitation of the hatched fly. Imitation of the natural, as closely as possible, was always seen as the key to success.

Let Nature guide thee; sometimes golden wire
The shining bellies of the fly require....
Each gaudy bird some slender tribute brings,
And lends the growing insect proper wings:
Silks of all colours must their aid impart,
And every fur promote the Fisher's art....
So just the colours shine through every part,
That Nature seems to live again in Art.
                              John Gay, 1713.

Medieval church wall painting (by kind permission of Fred Buller)

Precise imitation not a new thing

Exact imitation has been going for a very long time. In the *Treatyse of Fysshynge wyth an Angle* (1496), the fly that is described as appearing in March, whose imitation is to be tied with "donne wolle and the winges of the pertryche", is quite clearly the adult, hatched March Brown. No other fly with speckled wings and a dun body hatches in March. It is the first really noticeable fly of the season and the only one to have a defined hatching period of its own. So right back at the beginning of things we have a clearly defined fly species that the fly fisherman has been specifically imitating to catch trout, for over half a millennium.

There is evidence all over the place that the early fly fishermen were trying to imitate the hatched and floating fly with a floating imitation. William Samuel talks about fishing the floating fly for dace in 1577, and hints at its use for trout. Leonard Mascall speaks of

The True March Brown, *Rhithrogena germanica*

angling "aloft on the water," and refers to flies made with cork, in 1590. Gervase Markham, in 1614, again refers to flies made with cork; and even more importantly, instructs the fly fisherman to lay live captured flies in front of him and use his art to imitate their shape and colour. Robert Venables in 1662 said that artificial flies should be fished like naturals – "upon or above the water." And James Chetham, in 1681, used cork again, for fly bodies.

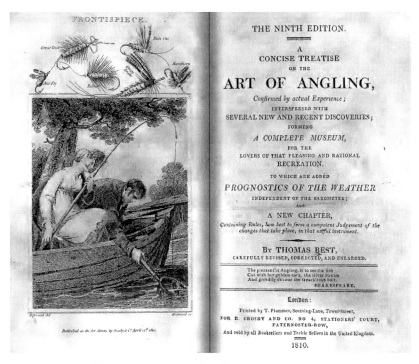

THE NINTH EDITION.

A
CONCISE TREATISE
ON THE
ART OF ANGLING,

Confirmed by actual Experience;

INTERSPERSED WITH
SEVERAL NEW AND RECENT DISCOVERIES;

FORMING

A COMPLETE MUSEUM,

FOR THE
LOVERS OF THAT PLEASING AND RATIONAL
RECREATION.

TO WHICH ARE ADDED

PROGNOSTICS OF THE WEATHER
INDEPENDENT OF THE BAROMETER;

And

A NEW CHAPTER,

Containing Rules, how best to form a competent Judgement of the
changes that take place, in that useful instrument.

By THOMAS BEST,
CAREFULLY REVISED, CORRECTED, AND ENLARGED.

The pleasant'st Angling, is to see the fish
Cut with her golden oars, the silver stream
And greedily devour the treach'rous bait.
SHAKESPEARE.

London:

Printed by T. Plummer, Seething-Lane, Tower-Street,
FOR B. CROSBY AND CO. NO 4, STATIONERS' COURT,
PATERNOSTER-ROW,
And sold by all Booksellers and Tackle Sellers in the United Kingdom.

1810.

Thomas Best's *The Art of Angling* first published 1787

The new idea of fishing upstream

Floating flies were fished, mainly downwind and on fixed lines, throughout the 1700s, and towards the end of the century we start to get more consistent advice to fish upstream, the idea having been in fact first publicised by John Worlidge as early as 1675 (below). By 1857 W C Stewart in *The Practical Angler* was recommending upstream dry fly fishing as the default practice so that a shorter line could be cast, the flies kept drier, the trout taking more confidently,

the Water-side as you can, and fish down the stream. In a swift stream where the bottom is hard, and not too deep, if you go into the middle of it and cast your Fly up against the Stream, the Trout that lies upon the Fin in such strong Currents, and discerns you not, being behind him, presently takes your Bait.

In March, April, and September, and all the Win-

and being hooked more securely – this coming after the dry fly had been made to sink too much by the tackle advances of the previous century (see below).

Richard Bowlker (soon to be edited – and followed – by his son Charles), in many editions of *The Art of Angling*, from 1747 to 1826, marked the start of modern fly-dressing. All of his flies were intended to float, and he fished to individual fish, casting a yard above the fish and "letting the fly move gently towards him, by which means he will show it more naturally." The upstream dry fly was well established, as at least a good technique to use, by the start of the 1800s.

Golden Ages for fly and fish.

Hatches were, in general, fabulous by comparison with today, and there is no doubt that these were golden ages in which fly was abundant and so were fish. Success in imitating the fly was considered crucial, and the size, colour, floatability, and presentation of the fly was well appreciated and turned to great effect in catching fish in scenarios where the hatches were voluminous and reliable – and imitation of the hatched fly therefore made total sense.

Lots of fly and lots of fish, taken together with the third factor of there being only a tiny population of people with the leisure to flyfish, also meant that there was little to drive development of new ideas in the pastime. I

under the but of the wing : as it swims down the water, its wings stand upright upon its back, its tail is forked, and the colour of its wings: it comes upon the water about eleven o'clock, and continues on till two, appearing on the water in shoals, or great quantities; in dark gloomy days, at the approach of the least gleam of sun, it is amazing to see, in a moment's time, the surface of the water almost covered with ten thousands of these pretty little flying insects, and the fishes rising and sporting at them, insomuch that you would think the whole river was alive; it is a pleasing sight to the angler, and affords him great diversion; in this manner they appear on the water every successive day, till the end of their duration. The blue dun, and the brown, are both on at the same time, the blues are most plentiful in

Abundance of fly, late 1700s, Thomas Best.

hesitate to call it a sport, in relation to those times: it was a leisure pastime for the relatively well-to-do. And it could afford to be a little bit lazy. The poetry and the illustrations show it to have been so. There was little competition, much concern that one's colleagues and companions should enjoy themselves, and a total absence of wannabes chasing their Personal Bests, at least until well into the 1800s.

A CATECHISM OF FLY-MAKING,

By WILLIAM BLACKER.

Question.—What do you mean by Fly-making?

Answer.—I mean the artificial assimilation of those beautiful insects that appear on brooks and rivers during the summer season.

Q.—What are these artificial flies used for in general?

A.—They are principally used to afford gentlemen rural amusement and recreation, by their taking both trout and salmon with the rod, line, and fly.

(Above) Amusement and recreation for gentlemen, as late as 1843, and 1859 (right, on the Hampshire Bourne)

Augt 9 · 1859 , I cast my first fly on the Hurstbourne water in my old fashioned Devonshire way, — saw thousands of fish, — and they saw me.

But then things changed, changed a lot, and changed really quite fast ...

Long lines, and reels, by 1800

Although reels did not come into common use until the end of the 1700s, there had been winches from much earlier times and Thomas Barker mentions the reel first, in his book *The Art of Angling* published in 1651. Barker was also the first writer to give detailed instructions on how to proceed with the dressing of a fly, and advised "fine fishing" with the fly riding high on the water. By the start of the 1800s however, reels seem to be in normal use and were probably, in effect, in semi-mass production.

Robert Salter, writing circa 1800, clearly implies a reel when he talks about your line needing to be 12 yards long with a leader of up to 3 yards on the end. William Shipley, writing in 1838 but from his father's diaries and notes which dated from the last quarter of the 1700s and the first quarter of the 1800s in Derbyshire, again refers clearly to "a reel-line of 20 yards in length" and recommends against pure silk which at that time could not be waterproofed and would get wet, overload the rod, and sink both itself and the fly. Bainbridge, publishing his *Fly-Fisher's Guide* in 1816, strongly recommends against the multiplier but implies reels were normal. Sir Humphry Davy, writing in 1828, but in relation to a fishing trip on the River Colne in 1810 has the following snatch of conversation between the learner Poet and the experienced Angler:

Poet – "I have him! Alas! He has broken me, and carried away half my bottom line. He must have been a fish of 7 or 8 pounds. What a dash he made! He carried off my fly by main force."

Angler – "you should have allowed your reel to play and your line to run: you held him too tight."

Split wing, cocked dry flies by around 1800.

Split wing dry flies were in common use in Derbyshire and right across England wherever anglers were imitating the hatched fly, long before the so-called Dry Fly Revolution came to pass at the end of the 19th century. David Foster from Ashbourne in Derbyshire claimed (later) to have invented the split wing cocked dry fly in 1833. James Ogden, his competing tackle manufacturer and dealer in Cheltenham, also with a Derbyshire base, claimed to have invented it in 1839. But in fact, Shipley's book of 1838 gives detailed instructions as to how to tie the split wing taken from his father's notes dating back to the 1780s in Derbyshire – this is not proof, but makes it likely that a pair of

David Foster

wings fixed upright, divided by the silk and supported by several turns of hackle placed under the wings and in front of a dubbed body was what formed the go-to dry fly about a century earlier than the Dry Fly Revolution, as it is normally referred to. And indeed, G C Bainbridge, in *The Fly-fisher's Guide* in 1816, gives clear instructions as to the mounting and splitting of upright wings. John Younger, fishing the Tweed and tributaries, does the same in 1839 in *On River Angling for Salmon and Trout* and adds the idea of taking pairs of wings from matching left and right wings from the donor bird, the technique claimed by Marryat & Co on the chalk streams forty years later. He, incidentally, was an early writer to deal with the problem of "the selective trout", although the subject had been briefly mentioned in 1806 by Alexander Mackintosh in *The Driffield Angler*.

With respect to the use of the dry fly, not specifically split-winged, George Pulman in *The Vade Mecum of Fly-Fishing for Trout* published in 1841 at Axminster in the West Country, recommends a dry, light, buoyant fly, showing that the use of the dry fly had

9. If ever you observe the trout rise short, and refuse your bait, you may be assured that it is not exactly the color of the fly that they took it for; such are their discriminating powers, that if it varies but a shade from the color of that fly which they are in search of, they will, when the water is clear, refuse it; from which you will readily infer, that it is necessary an angler should devote some portion of his leisure, to study the dispositions of that part of the " finny race," that he selects for his recreation ! yet by a little attention to the directions that these letters contain, you may soon become sufficiently acquainted with the nature of this amusement, to insure yourself a day's success when the elements are not unfavorable.

Robert Salter on Selectivity and the need to match the natural exactly by close observation spread also to the West Country by the 1840s. And on the Wandle in Surrey, hitherto unpublished diaries record Gilliatt Hatfeild in the same year of 1841 deliberately casting a dry Hare's Ear Dun and catching otherwise unresponsive trout.

The definitive book for the flyfisher's imitation of the fly

1836 saw the publication of Alfred Ronalds' superbly researched book *The Fly-fisher's Entomology*. This was the first, and for many years the only book to place first-rate, coloured engravings of the natural and of its artificial imitation side by side so that the angler could see the tricks he had to master (Halford himself later failed to do so).

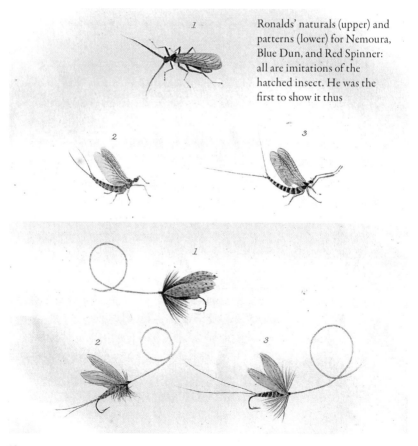

Ronalds' naturals (upper) and patterns (lower) for Nemoura, Blue Dun, and Red Spinner: all are imitations of the hatched insect. He was the first to show it thus

Ronalds knew his fly. His research was not just entomological however, but extended to trout behaviour, especially how they feed and how they react to flies both natural and artificial – he built an observation pod over the Blythe, his Staffordshire river, and spent hours, days and weeks in it watching the trout and the fly, and conducting experiments. (See the footnote on Alfred Ronalds' book at the end of the book for a picture of this). Both his suggested imitative tyings, and his advice in terms of method, were better and more useful than any that had previously been written. He, like Shipley, had no commercial interest to promote, and wrote simply to carry the science forward and share it with brother anglers in the most useable way. He made a collection of specimens, but as the technique of preservation in fluid was not yet developed, it was a pinned and dry collection. It is still in existence, in the Oxford Museum, but has been in a sorry state ever since it was bequeathed there on Ronalds' somewhat puzzling emigration to Australia.

First ever known emerger (and weighted nymph) patterns.

The earliest emerger imitation I can find is the extraordinary and explicit pattern illustrated by William Blacker (*Blacker's Art of Fly Making*, 1843 – see overleaf). In this the nymph body is shown separately from, but attached to the body of the dun. His instructions make it clear that this was a fly with two bodies and that the trout should see it as such.

My picture of a half-emerged BWO (below) makes it clear how

Winged Larva

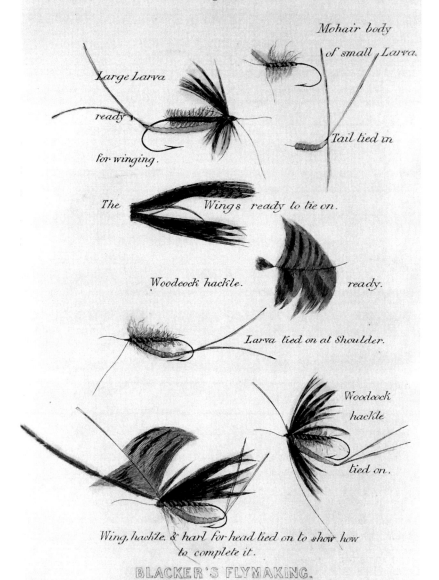

Mohair body of small Larva.

Large Larva ready for winging.

Tail tied in

The Wings ready to tie on.

Woodcock hackle. ready.

Larva tied on at Shoulder.

Woodcock hackle tied on.

Wing, hackle, & harl for head tied on to show how to complete it.

BLACKER'S FLYMAKING.

explicit that appearance of two bodies is in a crippled, swamped, or 'stillborn' emerger. And he twice recommends it for use on windy days and says it will do best where a strong rapid stream runs into a deep pool – i.e. when and where drowned emergers will be most plentifully available to the fish. This is very early, very good observation of trout food availability, carried through to fly design and to specific recommendations for presentation. Analysis of other and much earlier writers in the last half of the 18th century and the first half of the 19th shows that several of them (for example Richard and Charles Bowlker, and John Younger) were entirely appreciative of how the dun got to be on the surface – from below, not from above – and of the imitative opportunity afforded by this. Nor were they the first: knowledge of the nymphal form of flies had been not only been understood, but exploited with imitations a century earlier than that. Robert Venables describes the weighted caddis and how to

fish it in the 3rd edition of *The Experienced Angler*, 1668; and in 1681 James Chetham in *The Angler's Vade Mecum* describes using a horsehair line dyed dark but with the tip white to detect subsurface takes.

> is a moſt excellent Bait for a *Trout*. You may if you pleaſe place a ſmall ſlender Lead upon the ſhank of your Hook to ſink the Bait where the River is not violently ſwift, and draw the *Cadbait* over the Lead, you may make one the head of black ſilk, and the body of yellow wax; this you muſt be often raiſing from the bottom, and ſo let it ſink again.
>   You may imitate the *Cadbait*, by making the body of *Shammy*, the head black ſilk

Mail order tackle develops in the early 1800s – and generates fierce competition

The first Royal Mail mail coaches were introduced in 1784, and uniformed postmen were on the streets by 1793. The first dedicated mail train ran in 1830. In the meantime, the letter post was well-developed and packages could be effectively sent by courier services as now, although the official parcel post as such did not begin until 1883. The Penny Black stamp was introduced in 1840.

Fly lines and reels were now in mass production and could be advertised, sold and distributed nationally. Foster and Ogden had seen their opportunities, and being provincial did not have the London market on their doorstep to support their retail shops sufficiently, and so went for mass marketing by mail order via catalogues. They particularly saw the opportunity for marketing their flies, with their claimed superior design and construction. Most tackle was still sold by tackle shops, of course, but mail

order was where big opportunities lay, just as in clothing – where Halford's family was at this time building their business. Advertising and catalogues were the name of the game in both markets.

Premium prices for flies

By 1890 James Ogden, trading mainly by post, was sending out 700 dozen of his mayfly patterns, at 6/- to 8/- per dozen – not by any means a low cost item for the angler or a loss-leader to him, given that you could purchase his 'Multum-in-Parvo' rod ("over 10,000 sold") for one guinea: 21/-, only three times as much as his price for a dozen dry flies. Makes you think, now, a good carbon rod will cost you £500-£700 and a dozen flies from a top supplier £18: the cost of rods has rocketed relative to flies, and which is more important? Top quality split-cane trout rods did indeed cost from £2 10/- up to £6 10/-, but the relativities still favoured income from the fly, and this was a trade worth protecting from rivals at those prices.

Publicity, image building and competition

One method of advertising was to write your own book. James Ogden published *Ogden on Fly-tying* in 1879 and David Foster's sons, not to be outdone, published *The Scientific Angler* as a collection of his notes and papers after his death, in 1882. Prior to that, Foster himself had contributed a regular column *Notes on Angling* to "various newspapers", another method of gaining publicity.

These two men, and the London Tackle merchants, were facing a new competitor by this time, as Hardy's of Alnwick set up in 1872 and the brothers started selling fishing tackle in 1874, again nationally and via advertising and catalogues. Ogden's and Foster's books came decades later than their main selling thrust, (the former were selling dry

James Ogden,
with his short 8 ft 'Multum in Parvo' rod

flies with upright split wings in 1854) and may well have been partly in reaction to Hardy's energetic marketing from 1874 onwards.

Competitive and protective reputation-building was now the name of the game, and had been for 20 or 30 years. Shipley writing in 1838 with no commercial interest to promote other than his father's memory, referred fairly bitterly to those involved in the tackle trade with the following words:

> "...the irritable, and, I fear, enviable race of anglers by trade – a race remarkably constipated when they are asked their opinion of the merits of a rival, or when they are asked for any useful information relative to their craft, lest, by freely giving it, they may injure their own reputation..."

Dry Fly Only rule starts in Derbyshire in 1865

The dry-fly-only rule is often mistakenly attributed to the Southern chalk streams, but the first dry fly self-flagellants were not in the south – they were in Derbyshire on the Haddon Hall water of the lower Wye, in 1865. And indeed they are still there today, and have gone even further in sackcloth and ashes than the most purist adherents to the dry fly on the Test and Itchen, since they refuse to accept the Klinkhamer or any parachute-hackled fly as a dry fly. When their collar-hackled dry flies sink into the surface film as far as or further than any Klinkhamer, the fly is still considered dry, no matter that it cannot be imitating the dun. No emerger patterns at all are allowed, however high-floating – day ticket purchasers are constrained to read pages of rules before fishing. It was, strangely, James Ogden who was responsible. He went back to his native county in June 1865 to fish for a few days, and found the locals all fishing the dap with live mayflies. He showed them his straw-bodied artificials worked even better (a local commented, "if he'd not fallen in, he'd have caught every fish in't'watter") and the Steward for the Estate imposed the artificial dry fly rule next day, with near-riots resulting.

Distance casting trumps flotation

It might seem a bit weird, but in actual fact dry fly fishing was, by the 1870s, in trouble. There had been, over the previous forty years, successive arrivals (and enthusiastic uptake) of innovative tackle – shorter more powerful rods of cane and greenheart; silk lines that you could cast long distances with; reels that enabled you to shoot and recover line; and gut casts that were thinner and stronger than the equivalent in horsehair, monofilaments which had to be pre-soaked for safe knotting, and hence sank. Shorter and stiffer rods like James Ogden's 'Multum in Parvo' (much power, small rod) enabled the angler to cast into the wind when it came downstream at him, and no longer to have to present a floating fly downwind. However, all these individually brilliant improvements taken together meant that the floating fly with which you hoped to imitate the natural, didn't – it sank. So actually it is true that by 1850 many people were, perforce, using wet, those flies that were originally designed to be fished dry – and up until then, had been.

A revealing article in *The Field* in 1853 entitled *The Hampshire Fly Fisher* poured cold water on fishing upstream, saying "as far as fly fishing is concerned, fishing upstream, unless you are trying the Carshalton dodge and fishing with a dry fly, is very awkward" from which we may conclude that upstream fishing with the dry fly was already established on the Wandle at that time, and had been tried but found wanting in Hampshire. Halford started his trout fishing on the Wandle in 1868.

Sinking in the bursting flood

After getting on for 400 years of the First Age of Flyfishing flowing in its narrow channel, this Second Age from say 1770 to 1870 was bursting out to overflowing with flyfishing development, but an age in which the dry fly had progressively got compromised by better delivery tackle. Huge improvements had been made in rods, reels and lines as we have seen. Anglers could cast great distances using them. But the presentational abilities of the earlier close-to fly fisher were more than halved as his casting distance was doubled, and his old-style flies (designed to be fished downwind) sank, and needed to be redesigned to float by themselves and to be fished upstream. The sea was running out, as it were: but the Third Age was coming on apace, and it would be a tsunami of change.

Fertile ground, and green shoots

130 years ago at the time of writing, the period centred on the year of 1884 when The Flyfishers' Club was founded, was characterised by a firework display of new ideas, new happenings, and new achievements in the trout flyfishing arena. Exciting things were also happening for coarse fishermen and for salmon fishermen, but it was the trout fishermen who were seriously getting their act together and putting on a show the like of which has arguably never been repeated.

ONE SHILLING

GREAT
INTERNATIONAL
FISHERIES
EXHIBITION

OFFICIAL CATALOGUE

LONDON
1883

WILLIAM CLOWES & SONS LIMITED.

1883 saw the hugely successful International Fisheries Exhibition at Crystal Palace which drew in total 2.7 million visitors at the rate of 20,000 a day (you might contrast this with the piddling footfall at Fishermen's Row at the Game Fair nowadays). This gave oxygen to the development of all kinds of fishing, and flyfishing in particular was ready to breathe it in and swell its lungs.

The general context was one of burgeoning ideas, technical facilitation, and literary innovation.

Technical breakthroughs bring critical mass

Over the previous four years, Hall had perfected an eyed hook which meant that the fly fisherman could change his flies, and adjust the thickness of his gut more freely; and Turle had invented the Turle knot, enabling up-eyed hooks to be tied on straight. The advanced method of tying the double split-winged floater had been developed by Marryat, and refined by himself, Sanctuary, and Hall working together; and they had cascaded this know-how into the brain, fingers, and family of Holland, the already well known commercial fly dresser. Holland had been tying flies commercially in Manchester, and Halford, Hall, Marryat and Sanctuary brought him down and set him up in Salisbury to serve them and the new chalk stream dry fly fishermen – a win-win arrangement. Halford was by now a central mover and shaker in this group, and was already setting about the codification of imitative flies with eventual publication in mind (1886, the much-trailered *Floating Flies and How to Dress Them*).

Although, as I have argued in my book *Flyfishing outside the Box: Emerging Heresies,* this imitative locomotive almost immediately diverted itself onto the particularly pretty branch line of dry fly purism, the steam and piston-thump that it got up as it left the station was astonishing, and the coaches that it pulled behind it were full of cheering crowds of fly fishermen.

Everything was going for flyfishing at this time.

Companionship in sport

Major flyfishing clubs had been started with the provision of water as their main aim (for example the Hungerford Fly Fishing Club later to become the Wilton FFC, the Piscatorial Society, the Houghton Club, the Yorkshire Fly-Fishers' Club, and so on). Many of the big hitters in the fly fishing world were involved in setting up these clubs – for example W H Aldam from as far away as Derbyshire (the editor of *A Quaint Treatise on Flees, and the Art a Artyfichall Flee Making*) was the main publicised backer of the Wilton Fly Fishing Club (of which I am now President) and on its move in 1890 from the Kennet to the Wylye, H S Hall, the eyed hook and split-wing dry fly exponent, joined it as an influential member (see John Knott's *History of the Wilton Fly Fishing Club,* 2013).

Spending power – the aspidistra pound.

The new upper-middle-class was expanding rapidly and gaining rapidly in disposable income and in leisure time, fuelled by the success of Victorian modernisation and the development of mass production

and mass markets. Halford himself was a case in point, his wealth assured and his early retirement into a fishing career funded by his family's immense success in supplying mass-produced clothing to the upwardly mobile and the aspirational (their Oxford Street store, pictured right).

It was this very economic sweet spot which had created the Hyam/Halford business fortune, based on the national advertising, catalogue marketing, mass production, and highly successful mass sales of aspirational clothing. (We shall not speak of the imperial, and indeed local British, sweated labour involved).

His own branch of the family had a great big factory in Leeds and a very large shop on Oxford Street. Their nationally-distributed catalogue, *The Gentleman's Illustrated Album of Fashion*, was an institution in the 1850s and 1860s, before switching to heavy newspaper advertising for self-measured mail order, or for visiting one of the their many provincial outlets. (I don't expect that most of his flyfishing colleagues even knew that, but I bet that as a lawyer and an inveterate investigator, Skues did. Skues by contrast had to work for his living until he was over 80).

The icon of the gentleman

The middle classes had been created and enriched by Victorian commercial success right across the industrial and consumer spectrum, and their members were upwardly mobile and highly aspirational – to be gentlemen. Angling as a distinctive pursuit of gentlemen was an idea given authority from the earliest times: Wynkyn de Worde, the

Westminster printer, describes the new edition of the *Treatyse* (1496) as "a compendyous treatyse of fysshynge wyth an angle, whiche is right necessary to be had in this present volume: by cause it sheweth afore the manere of hawkynge and huntynge wyth other dyvers maters right necessary to be knowen of noble men and also for it is one of the dysportes that gentylmen use."

This new spending-power carried the growth of flyfishing in its comet tail, and freed up the great Victorian ideas men to think – general naturalists like Darwin, entomologists like the Reverend A E Eaton – and Halford. There was prejudice against commercially successful Jewish incomers, and Halford was not alone in setting out to build an unassailable reputation in a distinctly British sphere – another good example was Ludwig Messel, who used gardening as his way into the upper echelons of Victorian and Edwardian society, creating Nyman's and throwing a procession of garden parties there and across a dozen other local gardens.

Responsive angling media develop

By now many experienced and influential authors were writing books and contributing regularly to periodicals such as *The Fishing Gazette* and *The Field*. *The Fishing Gazette* in particular, launched in 1879, was weekly and voluminous, and now a collector who has every copy on his shelves needs a very long library wall to house it. It was not very different from a combined blog and forum: and being weekly it was almost as immediate to the reader – it was widely leapt upon and devoured by anglers in those pre-radio,

Francis Francis

RB Marston

pre-TV days. And *The Field* was already by then a source of information about dry fly fishing – H S Hall wrote that in 1874 or 1875 he had been drawn, by articles in *The Field*, to Winchester to experience the single dry fly technique on the Old Barge water for the first time.

These authors and their editors (Marston at *The Fishing Gazette*, Francis Francis, followed by William Senior at *The Field*) were at least as influential as the technical and field developers of the sport were at that time, in fact even more so. In addition to these, H. Cholmondely-Pennell, 'John Bickerdyke' (C H Cook), and Alfred Jardine were typical of the period's writers, and were soon to be joined by Halford himself.

More trout, by any means

Incidentally, although many of these people had been brought up on wild trout fishing, the majority of them were not committed to it, and it was part and parcel of the whole idea of the growth and development of flyfishing for trout, that wild stocks should be augmented right up to the estimated carrying-capacity of each water by farm-bred fish. Indeed there was a major industry already developed to supply these stockies, from the Loch Leven trout farm to the High Wycombe trout farm that had already, 20 years previously, supplied trout eggs to Australia and New Zealand.

Halford and his coterie were complete believers in stocking, and it was not until much later that the disastrous experiences of Ramsbury, Abbotts Barton, and the Bourne finally demonstrated that stocking destroys wild trout fishing. Not that many fishery owners took much notice. Skues was one of the few who opposed the practice, which, when you think about it, compromises the whole idea of imitation as the key to the sport, insofar as a stock fish is more likely to be deceived by an accurate imitation of a pellet.

The travelling angler

Physical access to fly water had seen an explosion as well, and travel by train was almost universal, the railway lines which Dr Beeching later axed largely following river valleys so as to avoid uneconomic uphill climbs. At that time, London fly fishermen were able to fish the Lea, the Thames and its tributaries (the Chiltern streams, the Wycombe Stream, the Colne, the Chess, the Pang, the Lambourn, the Kennet to the North and West, and the Wandle, the Cray, the Darenth, and the Kent Stour to the South): and in addition all the Southern chalk streams (the Test, the Itchen, the Hampshire Avon, and all their tributaries). Derby and Burton anglers were easily able to fish the Trent, the Dove, the Blythe, the Manifold, the Wye and the Derwent, and similar access was possible for the anglers of Yorkshire cities and many other major urban areas. This physical access was all subject, of course, to the fishing being legally and financially available to the fly fisherman in one way or another – and at this time it was getting tied up tighter and tighter owing to growing demand and ability to pay.

So... by the 1880s everything was present in the fisherman's pie, the oven was pre-heated, and a glorious dish was in prospect.

An idea is conceived

One thing was felt to be needed – something to connect the disconnected elements of the sport's development, something to bring people together, both experts and tyros, both the brilliant fly casters and the brilliant fly tiers, the scientists and the sportsmen, the perceptive and the communicative, the leisured and the busy, the deeply experienced and those bursting with ideas.

What was in concept was a club – but a very different one. Not a local one, but a national one, even one with international links. Not a fishing club aiming to provide water. Not a club centred upon fishing competitions, or indeed upon any competition other than that between the fly fisherman and the fish. Hubbed in London (the centre of the known world) but with fast postal and train links to every part of the country.

This needed to be not just an organisational club, but a club with its own rooms where people could meet, and meet regularly (any day but more especially every Thursday night), to share experiences and ideas about flyfishing – and to form friendships, share information about, and find, good fishing.

Not just that, but accommodation in which could be collected and kept reference items and exemplars that could serve to show people the best possible tools and materials with which to go about their pursuit of fish with flies. And, of course, accommodation that could house the best flyfishing library in the world.

A short confinement for the club's birth

And that is how The Flyfishers' Club was born.

According to Basil Field, the founding President, the original prospectus described the club's purposes, voiced in the original prospectus of 1884, as follows:

> *To bring together gentlemen devoted to fly-fishing generally.*
> *To afford a ready means of communication between those interested in this delightful art.*

The Fishing Gazette.

SATURDAY, JANUARY 17, 1885.

A CLUB FOR FLY-FISHERS.

For some years past fly-fishermen have felt the want of a club where they could meet and discuss matters connected with their favourite sport. We are glad to be able to announce that this want no longer exists.

On the 18th of December last, several gentlemen well known in the angling world met together and unanimously decided that it was desirable to establish a club for fly-fishermen, and a committee was formed composed of the following gentlemen :—

John Brunton, M.D.	Alfred Jardine.
M. Burnett.	T. J. Mann.
H. Cholmondeley-Pennell.	Rev. J. Manley, M.A.
Henry Ffennel (*Land and Water*)	R. B. Marston (FISHING GAZETTE)
Edward Hamilton, M.D., F.L.S.	Wm. Senior (*Field*).
T. J. Hodson.	J. P. Taylor, hon. sec.

It was decided that the name of the club should be

THE FLY-FISHERS' CLUB.

"By this none maketh money—only contentment."

OBJECTS.

The constitution and purpose of the Fly-Fishers' Club, which is purely a social club (there will be no prizes or competitions), may be stated in brief to be :—

To bring together gentlemen devoted to fly-fishing generally.

To afford a ready means for communication between those interested in this delightful art.

To provide in the reading-room, in addition to the usual newspapers, periodicals, &c., catalogues and books, foreign as well as English, having reference to fishing, particularly to fly-fishing, so as to render the club a means of obtaining knowledge about new fishing places and vacancies for rods, and make it a general medium of information on all points relating to the art.

The annual subscription for London members is two guineas, and for country members* one guinea. There is no entrance fee at present. Although invitations to join the club have only just been issued, already most encouraging promises of support have been received from gentlemen in London and the provinces, and with such a strong committee there can be little doubt of the success of the club. An excellent "home" has been secured at 10, Adelphi-terrace, Strand (the old quarters of the Savage Club), overlooking the Thames Embankment gardens, and within three minutes' walk of the Charing-cross stations of the L. B. and S. C. and District Railways. The house belongs to the Caledonian Hotel opposite, and the members have all the conveniences of a good hotel at their disposal. There can be no doubt that fly-fishers resident in the country will see the advantages of belonging to a club frequented by fly-fishers, where they will find all the current literature on the subject, and where they can make appointments to meet friends. The regular meeting night is fixed for Thursday in each week. Fishing-tackle makers in all parts of the country are invited to send their catalogues, and also small neatly-framed cases of specimens of their flies for salmon, trout, and grayling, &c., with names attached. These will be hung on the walls for the convenience of members. Proprietors of waters who have vacancies for fly-rods are also invited to send particulars. All such communications should be addressed to J. P. Taylor, Esq., hon. sec., Fly-Fishers' Club, 10, Adelphi-terrace, Strand, London.

Gentlemen desirous of joining the club should apply to some member of the committee, or to the hon. sec., who will supply copies of the rules of the club.

* Only those will be eligible as "country members" who have [no fixed occupation in London, and do not live within ten miles of St. Paul's.

To provide in the reading-room, in addition to all the usual newspapers, periodicals, &c., catalogues, and books, foreign as well as English, having reference to fishing, particularly to fly-fishing so as to render the club a means of obtaining knowledge about new fishing places and vacancies for rods, and making it a general medium of information on all points relating to the art.

Smoking Room of the Flyfishers' Club, 1901
(No 8 Haymarket)

The midwives in attendance

The other prime movers were Francis Francis himself, for whom this had long been a dream, Senior, Halford, Cox, Gilbey, Turle, Carlisle, and Marston. Francis was now seriously ill, but had written in 1882 as Editor of *The Field* to a frequent contributor "I do wish someone would start a club, a real anglers club, where we simply met, dined and talked etc; but did not vulgarize it with fishing for prizes and all that rot. It would not be difficult. I should back it all I knew." It was Marston who got the ball rolling, and Marston became the first Treasurer. The club was established in December 1884, seemingly at the first, (and intendedly, preliminary) meeting.

Minutes of the club's general committee, 10 November 1938 – Founder of the Flyfishers' Club:

"Mr R L Marston has presented to the Club a letter dated 15 December 1884 written by his father Mr R B Marston addressed to Mr J P Taylor inviting him to attend a preliminary meeting to discuss the question of starting a Club to be called the Flyfishers Club. The letter is, so far as is known, the first piece of evidence substantiating the fact that Mr R B Marston was the Founder of the Club. The committee decided that this letter be suitably

framed and hung in the Club. The letter was handed to Mr R L Marston by Miss M K Taylor, daughter of the late Mr J P Taylor."

Outside the tent

Marryat (right) was asked by Marston if he would join the club but declined good-humouredly offering a wooden spoon prize for the tallest tale about a big fish. Shame his offer wasn't accepted: the current holder would be our Librarian David Beazley, who when asked what was the biggest trout he had caught, said he did not recall and asked the questioner how tall was the tallest woman he'd ever made love to.

Hirsuted and booted

When the first annual dinner took place a year later there were already 250 members. It must have been an impressive sight, to judge from a contemporaneous engraving of the Piscatorial Society's annual dinner of a year later – white tie and tails, and the patriarchal beard absolutely de rigueur. A couple of hundred cloaks in the cloakroom, not to mention the same number of top hats and canes. (See engraving overleaf.)

The annual Piscatorial Society Dinner

Collections mooted

The Chairman, Sir Ford North, suggested that the club should make a collection of artificial flies, an idea that Halford rather turned to his advantage and went on to pursue in his books, within his own rather circumscribed chalk stream arena, but one that Skues also turned his mind to in 1893 when he joined the club, before giving up the idea of a national collection of artificial flies as too daunting and settling for a collection of fly-dressing materials.

During the early 1880s over the period leading up to the formation of The Flyfishers' Club, down on the southern chalk streams the movers and shakers of the dry fly revolution were finding their niches, settling into them and jockeying for position. The main exception was Marryat, who didn't feel any need to establish himself or his oeuvre in the public eye.

Innovations and reputations

H S Hall, (below) however, had been trying to establish himself (and not George Bankart) as the prime developer of the eyed hook, most notably in two rather self-aggrandising articles in *The Fishing Gazette* in 1884. The arrival of the eyed hook on the scene was a crucial enabler of the dry fly revolution, so his part in it was something he no doubt felt it important to establish. Nonetheless it had been W H Aldam who proffered him and Bankart the idea of the eyed hook for artificial flies, and in fact it was not entirely new, having been invented in the Bronze Age. Aldam had produced the retrospective book *A Quaint Treatise on 'Flees, and the Art a'Artifichall Flee Making* in 1876, with 25 real flies and their materials showcased in it; and one, the Mayfly, on an eyed hook. Hall probably had ambitions to write about the new fly-tying methods before anyone else did, and he certainly had the knowledge and experience to do so. However Halford had much more time to write, and published first in 1886, swamping Hall's nascent reputation.

One thing that does seem to have been clearly established by the extensive researches of Simon Ward into the life of Marryat, is that it was he who first invented the new two-matched-pairs method of upright split winged dry fly tying, with the long-jawed bulldog forceps aiding the technique, rather than Hall. Marryat to Hall, November 1882:

"My Dear Hall, A slack morning, and the spirit moves me to discuss a new method of winging for eyed hooks. I have not practiced it long enough to say that it is quicker than the old,

I certainly think it is better, now—take 2 right wing feathers corresponding to the same 2 left wing feathers, which rake also, cut them down the side of the quill till you have four bands of fibre thus—place 1 on 2 and 3 on 4 so that the points coincide all down as 4 and 5 ..."

... it was a long, long paragraph. Albeit, as we have seen, G C Bainbridge, publishing *The Flyfisher's Guide* in 1816, gave clear instructions for the mounting and splitting of upright wings, and John Younger, writing in 1839 added the idea of taking pairs of wings from matching left and right wings from the donor bird. So Marryat's invention wasn't actually original.

Sanctuary was also trying to establish himself as an influential fly fisherman and, perhaps feeling that his behind-the-scenes collaboration with Marryat in developing new flies and fly-tying methods would not be sufficiently publicised, went about this a different way by, I'm afraid, falsifying diary evidence to claim that he had captured the British record grayling in 1883. When the grayling record was established by a River Test fish of 4 lbs 8 oz, he went back and falsified his diary to show that he had caught a 4 lb 9 oz grayling (actually 1 lb 9 oz) at Bemerton on the River Nadder (actually on the Wilton FFC waters on the Wylye) but did not change the date.

GRAYLING. 4 lbs 9 ozs.

The Diary of an All-round Angler (1949) of Patrick Smythe records the details of their fishing day together at Great Wishford on the Wylye on October 24th 1883 and keys precisely to the altered details in Sanctuary's own diary for that date – a 66-year posthumous conviction for the angler's lie. You can see it's been altered. Tony Hayter is the person who discovered this. Sanctuary's weasel-claim was made in *The Fishing Gazette,* 26 July 1913, where in referring to the Wiltshire Avon, Sanctuary wrote "In the latter stream, or rather in one of its tributaries, I once caught with a small dry fly a perfectly shaped and conditioned fish which weighed just over 4 1/2 lbs". The claim was accepted, and this picture postcard (opposite) from 1952 shows that the lie persisted even after Smythe's book was published.

As Marryat insisted on a back seat and Halford got the front one, Hall and Sanctuary faded from public prominence, eclipsed by Halford's work.

Halford makes imitation his own

Halford had played a master stroke in 1880 by taking rooms at Houghton Mill on the Test. This became established as a centre for 'aprés-pêche' discussion and development, and for fly-tying for the chalk streams, and it was influential in his becoming accepted and established in the new dry fly group during the years before the Flyfishers' Club itself came into being in London. Tony Hayter has drawn attention to the first evidence of his specific interest in natural flies and their identification in his journal entries for 1880; and his interest in tying his own imitative flies also started about then. When Marryat taught Hall how to tie the new double split-wing floater in 1882, Halford would have been a contemporary student. Marryat was the source of all wisdom on this topic at the time, and 1881 was when Halford first started fishing frequently with Marryat.

Although there were clearly reputational issues, there is no evidence of anything other than friendly co-operation between Halford and either Marryat, Sanctuary, or Hall: or indeed later between him and

A pre-double-split-wing dry fly
from Marryat's pre-1883 'portmanteau'

the non-purist Walker, or even between him and Skues – at least until 1904. Everything and everyone was in ferment during those early 1880s: but it was Halford who was ensuring that he got carried to the top of the vat, together with his ideas.

Marryat still un-tented

There seems to be no doubt that Halford, who fully acknowledged the part played by Marryat, asked him to co-author his first book (*Floating Flies and How to Dress Them*) which he was clearly already working on at the time of the foundation of the Flyfishers' Club – and that Marryat declined, just as he declined to join the new club. But later, after Marryat's untimely death, Halford destroyed all Marryat's letters and papers in his possession. This act, which dismayed Marston, left no chance of Marryat's true input ever being evaluated. Marryat's deep prior involvement with Hall in dry fly development, coupled with Hall's disgust with Halford's having upstaged him, may have increased his reluctance to co-author Halford's book. And in the intervening ten years, Marryat and Halford grew apart, although remaining friends – several seasons passed without their fishing together. Loyalties and friendships were already under stress.

A dry fly diaspora

So by the trout season of 1885, the Flyfishers' Club was fully founded in London, and the group of the leaders of chalk stream flyfishing had reached critical mass in Hampshire and Wiltshire.

By the start of 1886, imitative (dry only, please) dressings of natural flies were established on the southern chalk streams from the Lea westwards through the Thames tributaries to the Dorset Frome and back eastwards through the Avon, the Test, and the Itchen to the Kent Stour – and established as the *sine qua non* for the serious fly angler. Although the South trailed behind the rest of the country in its adoption of the dry fly, keen aficionados had been fishing it on the southern rivers for ten years by then, and by now the technique had taken root. The Wandle in Surrey was earlier into the use of the dry fly than Hampshire, and the 'Carshalton Dodge' (involving 'spreading': swishing the fly around in a figure-of-eight to dry it without cracking it off; with the added use of petroleum jelly to waterproof it) seems to have been established there since the 1850s. Halford's first book was now about to be published (in April 1886), with the (90) patterns already tied and being used to prepare the coloured plates.

Tying skills imported to the South Country

George Holland, the greatest fly dresser in the country, newly taught by Hall in an exchange of over 100 letters to tie the double split-wing cocked dry fly, with his skills refined by Marryat and Sanctuary, was now brought down to Salisbury from Manchester and installed next door to the latter two gentlemen in Crane Street, to supply the demand. Demand proved nothing short of explosive.

What had been established down in Hampshire, nested within the generality of

MR. GEORGE HOLLAND.

flyfishing, was a tightly-knit Jesuit-style seminary of dry fly purism. But back in London, although the same people were centrally involved and were very influential, the Flyfishers' Club was a very much broader flyfishing church and its leaders, no doubt with a view to avoiding putting off new members (and keeping the initial 250 on board) were concerned to keep it broad.

Advertisements featured at the end of the 1888 edition of James Tayler's *Red Palmer*

No nymphs please, we're British

Demand for imitative flies was indeed explosive and the commercial fly-tyers could not cope – but it was only for dry flies. The undertow pulling the exact imitation of subsurface trout food back out to sea was, and for over three decades was to remain, every bit as strong as the tsunami now rolling the exact imitation of hatched fly up the beaches and into the civilised world.

Apostates and heretics persist

They were by no means all completely committed to a religiously imitative approach, and the editors and writers at the top of the club failed to sign up with alacrity to Halford's purist ideas. Both Senior and Marston (actually its publisher) were, in their 1886 reviews of it, strongly critical of Halford's first book in terms of its insistence on using the dry fly only, and on addressing only rising fish. Jardine, Carlisle, and Dewar were other very influential people at the top of the Flyfishers' Club who were resolutely non-purists. Basil Field the inaugural President, even ten years later in 1894, was extolling the joys of taking a break from flyfishing to go tickling trout in the weed; and in 1897 he was aiding and abetting four members of the Committee to catch trout on a minnow, and telling the story at the Annual Dinner. But the pursuit of exact imitation was an idea gaining strength all the time, and already probably dominant where the flyfishing pot was boiling fastest.

Halford and Senior happily filling pipes ... and littering: but with what?

43

Do as I say...

Something that was later hushed up (as Halford decided that the only gentlemanly way of fishing for trout was upstream dry fly) was that Marryat and he, and others such as C E Walker had already been experimenting quite extensively with subsurface nymph imitations. In fact Halford and Marryat in the years they fished together made it their default practise to autopsy their fish, regularly disgusting their companions without compunction—and so Halford can have been in no doubt whatsoever of the facts of the matter—trout dominantly eat nymphs. When Marryat abandoned his enormous working fly wallet, the 'Portmanteau' in about 1883, in favour of a newly designed box containing only dry flies dressed by the new double split-wing method, the former (below) contained a pretty fair sprinkling of nymph patterns (it still does contain a few, although many have subsequently been purloined). But already now, in the late 1880s, the jesuiticals were intent upon the inhibition, and if they could the prohibition, of subsurface experimentation. So much so that Francis Francis, when a guest in the fishing hut at Houghton on the Test and perforce listening to purist diatribes, was moved to exclaim " I wish the dry fly had never been invented!"

Marryat's 'Portmanteau' – examples of nymphs and wets pre-1883

Sub-aquatic imitation steamrollered

Soon to become a victim of the dry fly tsunami, through literary and reputational eclipse was C E Walker, who in 1898 after much experimentation published his book *Old Flies in New Dresses*. In this he recommended the imitation of nymphs, shrimps, corixae and terrestrials (below), giving detailed tyings and flying in the face of Halford's increasing calls for dry fly purism. The dry fly revolution rolled over him although he was an imitative innovator of the first order. Walker had great designs for shrimps and corixae, and a general recipe for ephemeropteran nymph imitations in 1898. But who nowadays has even heard of his work?

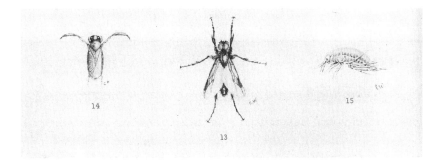

A 30-year confinement for the nymph

Skues, fifty years post-hoc, showed rather a good drawing of an upwing larva imitation he privately designed (but which, discouraged by the jesuiticals from pursuing, he did not publish) as early as 1888 using gut for the abdomen – and in 1891 he did actually publish a weird but realistic shrimp pattern in the *Fishing Gazette* – but no nymph pattern that looked like a real one saw the light of day until Mottram published in 1915. (Mottram was still enthusiastically using nymphs, including weighted ones, right through and including the period in the 1920s when Skues was finally getting his own exact larval imitations under way: he later recanted and disowned the nymph, but not until the opposition to Skues and the nymph built up in the latter half of the 1930s).

Skues himself did not publish or recommend a single actual nymphal imitation that really looked like one until 1908, and then it was another ten years before he produced one further pattern in 1918. As late as 1921, he was able to write meaningfully (in *The Way of a Trout With A Fly*) "I can cordially concur in the often expressed wish that some wet-fly enthusiast would set to work and make exact reproductions of nymphs and larvae in the same way as Mr F. M. Halford treated the floating fly." "Some wet fly enthusiast!" Heaven forfend that he should himself be thought to be one!

An attitudinal gaoling

It wasn't lack of observation, perspicacity, or thinking power that had thus far stopped Skues from doing that himself. It had been way back in 1888 at Abbots Barton that he had first taken a good look at the 'tiny pea green creatures' in the mouth of a newly caught trout, and designed his abandoned imitation using translucent gut. Three decades and more later, from 1921 onwards, Skues was off the blocks and running with his new imitative nymph patterns – but not until then. That was when he started using the marrow scoop and white plate to inspect what his fish had been eating (almost entirely nymphs he later said 'as always') – but he had been religiously if disgustedly conducting autopsies on his fish for over twenty years by then. During that whole period, he knew with perfect clarity what trout mainly ate, and what their subsurface food looked like – but was content with non-imitative subsurface flies (Northern spiders; wet flies with perpendicular wings; cut-down Tups fished wet, etc). Not really explainable except by reference to inhibition.

Inhibited... who, I?

The only real reason for this Great Nymph Lacuna, three decades without any serious, published nymph pattern development, sorry but it has to be said, was the dead hand of Halford and the inhibitions and prohibitions of his followers. So what was happening in the interim? Well, imitation wasn't dead – it was just limited to that of the hatched dun, and of the transposed spinner. Their exact imitation was pursued with extraordinary energy, vigour and science by Halford, first privately (in Hampshire and at home) and then within the Flyfishers' Club: together with a rolling small band of enthusiasts for as long as each could keep up with him (basically, only Mosely stayed the course). The way he did it was by persuading the club to form a Natural Fly Sub-Committee, with him at its head. But that did not come to pass until 1901, and meanwhile he had work to do.

Science-gathering

Whilst all this had been going on, amazingly good scientists, most of whose work stands little-altered today, such as Eaton and McLachlan, had described, identified and prepared taxonomies of the entire firmament of aquatic flies in all their life-stages. Halford was now studying their monographs closely. In 1886 he got stuck in to Eaton (below), McLachlan, and Pictet. He also joined the Linnaean Society, and started detailed correspondence and discussions with other members interested in aquatic insects. He became fascinated with the detail of aquatic entomology and with the potential for ever more precise identification of hatched duns and egg-laying spinners, leading

TRANSACTIONS

OF

THE LINNEAN SOCIETY.

I. *A Revisional Monograph of Recent Ephemeridæ or Mayflies.* By the Rev. A. E. Eaton, *M.A.* (*Communicated by Sir* John Lubbock, *Bart.,* F.R.S., *Pres. Linn. Soc.*)

(Plates I.–LXV.)

Part I. Read April 19th, 1883.

Introductory Remarks.

The present monograph is designed to facilitate the study of the Ephemeridæ. On

AN UNSCIENTIFIC ANALYTICAL SYNOPSIS OF THE GENERA OF BRITISH EPHEMERIDÆ

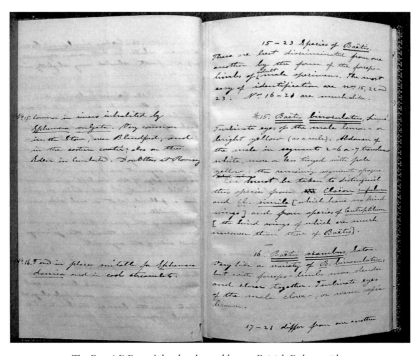

The Rev AE Eaton's leather-bound key to British Ephemeridae

to ever more exact imitation of them at the vice. Tony Hayter tells us in his definitive work *F M Halford and the Dry Fly Revolution* that Halford filled a fat notebook with his own and others' observations. From 1885 to 1888 he produced very many articles, and also his first two books – a very great deal of research, writing, design, and editing which must have taken huge amounts of his time.

In fact, in 1886, the Rev A E Eaton wrote out, longhand, a complete key to the Ephemeroptera specially for Halford, and this was bound in leather for him by a close friend named Daniels, and is still there in the Flyfishers' Club to be consulted. 37 pages long, plus 10 pages of references this is a work not just of scholarship, but of friendship : it is brimming with helpful notes.

Specimen-gathering

After soaking up as much as he could of the science, Halford moved on to collecting, identifying and examining specimens. On moving from the Test to the Itchen at Headbourne Worthy in 1889, he started performing autopsies on all the trout he killed. As a result, he cannot have remained unaware of the huge preponderance of larval food as opposed to hatched fly in the throats and stomachs of the fish. But to him that was not the point. Trout not rising to hatched fly were just not, at the time they were eating below the surface, appropriate targets. Not for a gentleman, anyway, not on a chalk stream.

He will, naturally, have mainly used the butterfly net to catch live specimens of the hatched fly, rather than the Victorian equivalent of the Surber Sampler and the 3 minute under-water kick-sweep for nymphs. His fly collecting was energetically prosecuted on the Itchen, then back at Houghton on the Test when he went back there for the 1892 season, and also on the Kennet at Ramsbury when he moved there in 1893, up until 1896.

In fact, during the 1890s Halford spent a great deal of time collecting specimens. We can deduce this from the fact that by March 1901 he had completed a full all-species collection, captured, identified, temporarily stored in alcohol and then permanently preserved in formalin in sealed 'watchglasses,' of all the upwinged flies on the Test as representing the chalk streams, in all of their adult life-stages and a few in nymphal form as well, hundreds of specimens. This collection he proceeded to donate to the Flyfishers' Club in March 1901, simultaneously with being invited to inaugurate, and be Chairman of, a new 'Natural Fly Sub-Committee'. The NFSC was to be dedicated to the further collection of fly exemplars from all the main flyfishing rivers of the UK as a guide for local and travelling anglers, and to illustrating the life cycles of important flies.

This was it for Halford – he really had arrived, and arrived in depth: as an author, a scientist, a practitioner, and an organisational leader. He was in every sense an authority. An authority, for Skues, was a *bête noir*.

Halford no slouch

As someone who has worked with scientists like Dr Cyril Bennett and Dr Peter Barnard , I know that it would be hard to over-estimate the time taken up in making such a collection, especially when looking for the rarer specimens (they are my learned colleagues, working to repair the Hun-bomb-damaged Halford Fluid Collection at the time of writing, and are people who do a great deal of insect collecting

– PB shown right working on the pinned sedge collection). The work takes years, not months. Tails break off the specimens in frequency directly proportional to their rarity and to the time taken to capture them. Even the industrious Halford must have

taken several years to complete this task. In fact I believe that he actually completed two collections, donating the best exemplars to the club and keeping the rest – and if I am right, it will have taken even longer...

High-spec preservation

In making these collections, Halford had by trial and error perfected the techniques for capture and encapsulation: interim preservation in one part of alcohol to 2 parts of formalin 2%, plus maximum dissolved menthol crystals; and permanent preservation in formalin 2% in solid 'watch glasses'. These latter were concave circular cells ground out of 2¼ in. square slabs of plate glass, filled with the preserving liquid and hermetically sealed with flat glass tops. One of the first things that the new NFSC did was to ratify the use of these methodologies for all further fluid collections. The makers of the watch glasses, F H Taylor and Sons of King's Cross, must have been delighted with the orders for hundreds of these that they got first from Halford and later from the Flyfishers' Club, but actually

that was their lot for some years, and when the club wanted to place a further order for a gross of them in 1909 they had gone out of business (the company actually failed three times, in 1899, in 1903, and in 1905). Somewhat surprisingly, they popped up again to supply the club from a new business base afterwards and were recommended by Mosely in his book of 1921 (might they have received some timely injections of capital?) and carried on until 1970.

If I may, I will suggest that we leave Halford and the NFSC for the moment at the point of their in inaugural meeting in March 1901, and return to them later. The reason for this is that some other very important things, both for the club and for imitative fly-tying, had been taking place in the meantime over the period of the 1890s.

The artificial side of things

Eight or more years before, Skues, who had already been reading widely in the literature, had had the idea of compiling *An Ideal Dictionary of Fly-dressing* (he said, in an article in the *Fishing Gazette* in 1893), but he rejected the idea in the end as being unachievable, as it would have been based upon obtaining flies from all over the country and he thought there would just be too many and they would be too hard to reduce to order in a useful concordance. So, at that time, and each in private, Skues and Halford were working up their ideas of making comprehensive collections – Skues one of fly patterns, and Halford one of natural fly specimens. Now this was the year, 1893, in which Halford put Skues up for membership of the Flyfishers' Club, their relationship was cordial, Skues was still in an admiring glow of *Floating Flies and How to Dress Them* and we may guess that they had been sharing their parallel ideas.

Not too long afterwards, in 1895, a sub-committee was appointed to form a collection of feathers and materials for fly making, of which the chairman was Marston and the secretary Skues. This sub-committee was however in charge of collecting materials, and not actual fly patterns as such. The minutes of the club's main committee in January 1896 record that this sub-committee presented a report and the report was discussed at considerable length at the AGM before the general committee approved its proposals.

Cabinet appointments

In December that year the main club committee recommended that a sum not exceeding £30 was to be made available to purchase a cabinet to be constructed to house the collection of fly-tying materials. In 1898 a quotation of £25 10s. 0d was accepted for the construction of the cabinet, and the

Adrian Kemp; at work on the Fur & Feather Collection

collection it was to be constructed for was now known as the Fur and Feather Collection. In 1898 a leading club member, Ohlson, who was also to be involved in the Natural Fly Sub-Committee asked that "some additional drawers be fitted to the Cabinet of fly-dressing materials as it was over full and many slides had been broken in consequence" – plus a notice requesting more care be taken. It does sound as if it was a popular reference collection.

The generosity of Skues

And in 1899 Skues stocked, and lent the club, an additional cabinet containing further fly-dressing materials. It was in that year also that his brother C A M Skues was appointed secretary of the club, a position he was to hold for many years. Even more materials space was added in 1902, when at the March meeting of the general committee Skues was authorised to purchase a cabinet for materials for tying trout (sic, ie not salmon) flies at a cost of not more than £7 10s. 0d. In

1904, Halford as President of the club, thanked Skues at the Annual Dinner for his hard work in building these collections of fly-dressing materials.

Prohibition – and no speakeasies allowed

But their relationship was already under strain. Halford was all up for exact imitation, and well under way in establishing what could and should be imitated, dominating the imitation arena in fact with the dry fly. But it was only imitation of the hatched fly that he was interested in.

Halford's natural fly collection funded for extension

In April 1900, the club's committee minuted receiving a donation of 20 guineas towards the expense of "housing and reclassifying a collection of natural flies." It was almost certainly Halford's own collection, or more likely as I think his duplicate collection, that was in prospect here – and it did not come with a cabinet, hence the necessary expenditure. The cabinet that would be needed, would have to be able to house the specimens in their watch glasses, and it is equally clear that Halford was thinking in terms of a cabinet with 18 trays each of 18 watch glasses.

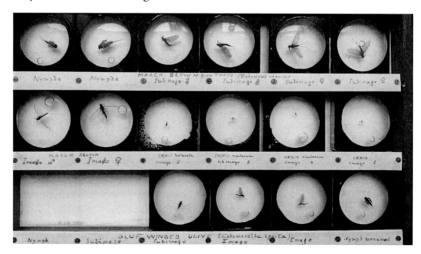

The Natural Fly Sub-Committee is formed

The donation came from Mr Harry Mear, and in 1902 an engraved plate thanking him and commemorating his gift was placed on the finished cabinet. He, naturally, became a member of the Natural Fly Sub Committee (hereinafter the NFSC) on its formation.

The NFSC held its first committee meeting at Halford's home, 6 Pembridge Place, on 29 March 1901, and the minutes of that and, patchily, of its subsequent meetings are still held by the club in the form of its minute book. There were six inaugural members including Messrs Halford, Ohlson, Mear, Walker (who had recently published his extremely non-purist book about non-upwing trout foods and their imitation), Lloyd and the secretary Kent.

They accepted the gift of Halford's collection of the Ephemeridae of the Test; they resolved to collect specimens of Ephemeridae (upwings) and Perlidae (stoneflies) from other rivers, especially from the north of the country; to have Halford initiate together with Morton, the scientific specialist, a collection of the Trichoptera (sedges); to have Walker contribute his Diptera (houseflies etc) and Corixae; and to commission a cabinet to house them all.

Early achievements of the NFSC

By March 1902 the Cabinet was in place, and a report of the work of the NFSC to date was to be prepared for the club's general committee. The life history of the Grannom in specimen form had now been included, together with the life history of the Alder fly, and the nymph and dun of the March Brown (The False, not the True March Brown as it turns out). In 1903 a life history of the Welshman's Button, the sedge *Sericostoma personatum* was added from the Test, the specimens bred in captivity from egg to adult by Gilbey's keeper

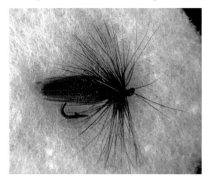

at Houghton on the Test – the later-famous William Lunn. This is sometimes wrongly identified as the Caperer, but the Caperer is *Halesus radiatus/digitatus* and is a much larger, although equally common across our rivers as a whole.

Martin E Mosely's pattern for the Welshman's Button, tied by him (by kind permission of Dr Peter Barnard)

The NFSC also in 1903 considered printing, for popular consumption so written simply, a series of life histories of all the most important anglers' flies: but I think this did not see the light of day. It is still something for the future.

"Go forth and multiply"

The next part of their plan was to get the club's members (especially the non-Test anglers) fired up to go and collect specimens from their own rivers, and send them in to the NFSC for identification and (possible) inclusion in the cabinet – but most importantly to form a database (a 'tabulation') of which flies were to be found on what rivers, and when were their appearance months. The idea was to guide anglers' expectations of fly species, what they were likely to find, and what imitations they would need to arm themselves with for success, whether they were locals or visitors to the rivers in question.

A big fat book of the recorded occurrences was what the NFSC had in mind, and that was in the end what they achieved, although only on a few (but important, see below) rivers were there dedicated enough fishermen to provide a complete (as far as could be judged) set of species.

The NFSC moaned quite a bit about the poor response from members, and made several attempts to gee them (and non-members via the *Fishing Gazette*) up with posters in the club, specially printed notices circulated, and so on. "Members as a whole not taking any active interest in the work of collection" was minuted. As nowadays, most members just wanted to go fishing, dammit.

Tablets of the lost Ark

The 'tabulation', both in its original handwritten form, and in the specially printed book form that was eventually presented to the General Committee in 1910, has been lost. Which is a shame, because it could now be used to present the Environment Agency, DEFRA, and Natural England, with incontrovertible evidence of local extinctions. (The point is, every specimen, to be counted, had to be identified by Halford, or later Martin E Mosely when he took over the NFSC – so no arguments can be allowed by today's supposed guardians of our ecology, to the effect that these old guys got identifications wrong or the records are old and cannot be relied on). Martin Mosely was another keen fly fisherman who educated himself to become an accomplished aquatic entomologist following in Halford's footsteps. He became one of the two top experts at the British Museum of Natural History and both researched and published widely. Their areas of interest dovetailed, with Halford being an expert in the Ephemeridae and Mosely fascinated by the Trichoptera.

The invertebrates went in two by two

Good data resulted, detailing which species were found, not just from the Test but also from the Itchen, Anton, Wylye, Kennet, and from the Wharfe: all these vouched-for appearances were included in the summary of the tabulated results that formed the Report of the NFSC that was published in the *Fishing Gazette,* January 1910, and which is thereby still available to the scientist and interested angler (this Report is attached as Appendix 1). And there is from the same basic source provided by FFC members' submissions, a complete tabulation of species from the Test and from the Dove in the Appendix to Mosely's book *The Dry-Fly Fisherman's Entomology,* 1921, which has I think not been appreciated for its potential usefulness by the regulatory authorities...not that the latter would want to know about it – too busy claiming that the UK's rivers are cleaner than ever. So the potential for mapping out local disappearances on these rivers remains, provided that good enough modern-day records can be found down to species level (the EA collected these, but has it kept them? Will the concerned scientists see them?)

We know numbers have fallen, but extinctions are more newsworthy and hence more useful as eco-ammunition.

There were incomplete records from 30 other rivers that were not included and have been lost.

In 1903 Halford was elected club President (having declined the honour a few years earlier on grounds of being too busy privately). This really was the final encomium. The club also accepted his gift of the manuscript of *Making a Fishery.*

A bit of a crisis?

At that point there is a gap in the minute book of the NFSC stretching a full five years to 1908. A page was cut out from the minute book following the minutes of the 1902 meeting, and the minutes of the 1903 meeting are written on a fresh page, over Halford's signature as usual. The fresh or replacement entry says "...that the members of the club as a whole were not taking any active interest in the work of collection (as suggested in the extract for *The Field*)"...And the importance of this work, and of following the necessary disciplines, was emphasised in the 1903 NFSC Report to the General Committee for publication to members.

During this time, in 1907, Mosely was elected to the club and also to the NFSC. In the next minutes, of May 1908, Halford was "the only surviving member" of the NFSC, and it had had to be reconstituted, although Kent was still the Secretary (so, more servant than master one suspects). Only one extra new member was appointed however, a Mr C K Reuss.

Oil and water

It was during this period, from 1903 to 1910 in fact, that Halford and Skues were disagreeing with each other about dry fly versus wet, in print and with increasing acrimony – sniping at each other's positions and work, in article after article in the angling press. (For the details, see especially Tony Hayter's book *G E M Skues: The Man of the Nymph*).

It will have been known for a little while that Skues was writing his first book (*Minor Tactics of the Chalk Stream* published in March 1910) and that it was not likely to agree with Halford's dry fly purism. Meanwhile, Halford was trying to get his intended *ne plus ultra* book *Modern Development of the Dry Fly* finished, with its definitive list of the 33 flies necessary and sufficient for the chalk streams, the 'Halford Series.' The list of flies was already published and was being used by the NFSC in communicating with club members and the world at large in 1910 (see Appendix below). But production problems, aggravated by the author's nit-picking, delayed publication of *Modern Development* for eleven months after Skues' book went on sale, albeit with the title page still bearing the date 1910. What Halford, or maybe both of them, had intended as a head-to-head publishing stand-off, dry to wet and wet to dry, turned into 11 months of advantage in which Skues got his ideas into the flyfishing arena.

Literary and personal daggers drawn: the stand-off

And it was probably in 1910 that Halford chose to tell Skues, in the Flyfishers' Club, that he was wrong (or it may have been 1911, which was when Skues said it was, in a 1946 letter).

Skues account of this was as follows (we have never heard Halford's side of the story):

'For some years prior to that I had been fairly intimate with Halford, but as my views widened with experience he became hostile and after publication of the book he took me aside and said, "you know, Skues: what you say in that book can't be done. Mind, I'm not arguing, I'm telling you." I replied "Halford! What good do you think you are doing by telling me anything can't be done which I have done scores of times." He got up and left me and never spoke to me again'.

Halford estranged?

Tony Hayter's view is that this argument actually went on for some time and was extremely bleak. He concludes that the two men avoided each other completely thereafter, and that it is even dubious whether Halford ever returned to the club's premises in Piccadilly – he certainly did not attend the annual dinners of 1911, 1912, or 1913, thus missing occasions on which Skues was praised for his work on the use of the wet fly. And the last meeting of the NFSC that he attended, on 29th of March 1910, was held at his house rather than at the club: although whether that was before or after the big argument with Skues we don't know. For Halford, the intervening years between his successes of 1903 and the argument with Skues had been unhappy, although his friends rallied round him. He withdrew from the club; certainly was not made unwelcome by the general membership although C A M Skues was Secretary and he may well have wanted to avoid meeting either or both brothers. Skues' review of *Modern Development*, published in 18th March 1911 issue of the *Fishing Gazette* ran to 3000 words, tackled Halford on just about every issue, and was uncomplimentary as well as critical. In July 1911, a gift of original flies tied by Skues was presented to the club and put on display, just as a set of Halford's flies had previously been given and accepted.

Mosely takes over

Getting back to the Natural Fly Sub-Committee, Halford had asked Mosely to take over the NFSC in 1907 after the sad death of his wife, following which he became depressed. Mosely did so with enthusiasm as is evident from all the reports that followed, until the 1930s. Peter Barnard, who has written Mosely's biography, says: "Mosely distributed specimen tubes to other members of the club, to encourage them to collect insects and send them to him for identification, and in the history of the club we read that 'Mosely deserves well of the Club, for he took his work *con amore* . . . his enthusiasm was unbounded' (Anon 1934). He also served on the General Committee of the Flyfishers' Club, and assisted the editor of the journal from its beginning in 1911 until 1931." Halford's son Ernest

Senior, Mosely and Halford

had married a cousin of Mosely's in 1895, so they were distantly related by marriage, but more importantly had by now been close fishing and bug-hunting friends for years.

First Cabinet half full – or still half empty

At the October 1908 meeting of the NFSC Mosely asked for and received approval to buy a further gross (144 for the non-duodecimal reader) of watch glasses and covers "to complete the present cabinet." There is no record of a new and further fluid/watch glass cabinet being ordered in the interim, and the glass makers had gone out of business as Mosely was soon to discover, so we have to conclude that this was still the cabinet delivered in 1902, as yet not full. The

Cabinet would hold 324 watch glasses, and the implication is that initially 10 drawers had been filled with 18 watch glasses each.

The cabinet plot thickens

In July 1909 the NFSC set about ordering a further, third cabinet to house a pinned, dry collection of ... (what exactly it was of is unclear, as Kent, the perhaps not-very-knowledgeable secretary left the word blank) There is still in the club, in a cabinet, a complete collection of pinned sedges, although the shock and vibration of the Hun Bomb of 1941 and of several premises moves has left many specimens separated from their abdomens to an extent that is not in practical terms repairable. However on the recruitment to the NFSC in 1909 of Henderson of Ashbourne, a keen supplier of specimens from the Dove, he was asked to undertake the making of this new pin collection, whatever it was intended to be. Since all the specimens in the extant pinned and dry sedge collection are clearly labelled in the minute and careful script of Mosely, who had been elected to the club and to the NFSC in 1907, I believe that the then existing and now still extant pinned sedge collection was his (and not one later formed by Henderson), and in fact Mosely is known to have donated a synoptic, overview dry collection of sedges to the club on his joining.

The club had already got, or soon would have, a pretty full and complete collection of upwings, stoneflies, selected sedges and other miscellaneous trout food items in fluid in a cabinet, and also an extremely comprehensive pinned collection of sedges in a cabinet. As mentioned above, this cabinet survives, and its exemplars are remarkable for a certain mummy-like beauty, and indeed for their very diversity: but they were much damaged by being blown up, and since there is not much distinguishing colour left in them, they are not of great use to the imitator: of potential use to scientists however, and a reference collection of national importance.

A change of mind by Mosely

Later the same year at the meeting of the NFSC in July, Mosely reported that no watch glasses could be sourced to complete the existing fluid collection; and he was, separately and explicitly, authorised to order a new cabinet for the prospective pinned collection. However, he seems by 1912 to have changed the *modus operandi* for the third cabinet from pinned to fluid (see below). Possibly, he had become aware at this time of Eaton's 1871 report on Ronald's collection in the Oxford museum which was pinned and dry, to the effect that it was by then in a deplorable state and worthless for identification purposes (much later, in 1930, Mosely visited it and published his own equally damning report, so we know he was aware of it by then).

Is the reader so far keeping up with these cabinets and collections? I am not sure the author is!

But it is pretty clear that by the end of 1911 there were three: dried and pinned sedges; anglers' flies in general in fluid watch glasses; and the (newly started by Mosely) fluid sedge collection. See Appendix 2.

No emergers please

Interestingly, the work of the NFSC during 1910 had included, in addition to the life cycle of the Dark Sedge *Notidobia ciliaris,* specimens showing the acts of eclosion, and of transposition of upwings, i.e. nymph to dun, and dun to spinner. This is the first and only mention of emergent fly, and we can be quite certain that it was not included as a model for imitation.

The Tablets of the Ark completed

Most importantly however, the 'tabulations' of all the flies from all the reported-from rivers had now been completed and delivered to the general committee *"in book form, and a suggestion that it should be placed in the club's Smoking Room for the use of members."* Enlarging on this, Mosely wrote in the first issue of the *Flyfishers' Club Journal*:

"in conjunction, therefore, they (the NFSC) tabulate the names of all insects sent in, and enter them in a book to be found on the Smoking Room table. Thus, if a member is desirous of visiting a special river he will eventually be able to turn up the river in question in this book, ascertain what flies prevail during the time of his visit, and then proceed to examine the actual flies in the cabinet, and either betake himself to the fly-tying room where he can make his patterns in imitation, or else match the insect and give his order to the local tackle shop."

A one page summary of the results of the tabulation, relating the naturals to Halford's final list of 33 flies, was published in the *Fishing Gazette* January 15th 1910, masterly in its conciseness (see Appendix 1). This covered the rivers Test, Itchen, Wylye, Anton, Kennet, and Wharfe. In April 1911, in the first edition of the *Flyfishers' Club Journal*, Mosely published a general report of the NFSC's work, and appended the newly-compiled lists of flies found and authenticated for the Dove and the Usk.

British Board of Fly Censors: Adults Only

The publication of these tabulations was an amazing achievement, and there is no doubt of Mosely's crucial involvement allied with the driving force of Halford himself, in making it happen. It was all done with specimens of duns and spinners – seemingly, 'no nymphs were harmed in the making of this programme.' It seems to have been an absolute rule that only hatched fly were to be captured and sent in. The first cabinet, the main Fluid collection that was donated by Halford and dated from before his dry fly fixation, does contain, it has to be said, the nymphs of most species. But subsequently, nymphs were delisted from all collecting.

Heady pre-war days

There followed, in the summer of 1911, a great flurry of submissions of specimens, from 9 collectors in total and from 15 rivers from the Aberdeenshire Don to the Dart, reported in the second issue of the FFJ. Further submissions were reported in the next issue of the Journal, and these now included flies from the USA and Norway. Mosely expressed the hope that the Latin names were now becoming so familiar that the old anglers' names for the flies would soon fall out of use. A scientist's transient dream that I am afraid serves mainly to show how out of touch with the average fly fishermen these enthusiastic experts had got.

The NFSC in wartime

Then, however, there were no more Journal reports from the NFSC until 1916.

Halford had died in the early spring of 1914, and the Great War started, but the work on natural flies went on, to good and detailed effect under Mosely's tutelage. In the FFJ of spring 1916, he reported much work on the rarer ephemeroptera, and also on Chironomids from Blagdon as the lake fly men got started (Sheringham was the source there). In addition, the Halford-Marryatt snail collection had been added; as well as the J C Mottram weed collection (below), following a very full article by him on weeds in the January 1915 issue, both in fluid form.

Halford's definitive instructions for preservation in fluid were recycled into the notice of members in this issue with a reprint of his article in *The Field* of 15 years before. There was a comprehensive and informative article by Mosely on stoneflies in 1915 also, with him making the point that several species are common on the chalk streams, but under-appreciated by chalk stream anglers.

The Winter issue of the FFJ, 1916-17 found Mosely in the army, and contributing a fairly light-hearted article entitled *In the Ranks*. There is nothing further from the NFSC until a personal article from Moseley about collecting, in the Spring 1920 edition, giving his own home address as the place to send specimens to. However, in the same issue, a letter of briefing and request to members appears over Kent's name as (still) Hon Secretary of the sub committee, asking for two different kinds of submissions:

a) For those unsure of precise identification, flies identified by the sender according to Halford's 33 patterns as previously promulgated in the reports, and
b) For those keen and knowledgeable enough, flies precisely identified for entry into the exact scientific tabulation that the NFSC was still keeping.

The club in wartime

The War carried with it tensions as well as sorrow from the losses of members and their sons:

10 June 1915 – A lengthy discussion following a member's complaint that the steward had been rude to him and should be dismissed, a fact the steward admitted but claimed extreme provocation. The committee agreed with him, and both the Steward and the member were reprimanded.

In the club premises, the Minutes of the General Committee reveal an involvement in the actual nitty-gritty not just of fly making, but of rod construction as well:

17 February 1916 – The Secretary reported complaints from several members as to the use of the Library + Passages for the making of bamboo about 24 ft long into salmon rods and varnishing them.

Lighter moments intervened as well:

25 November 1915 – Mr R B Marston's stuffed trout with two tails had been delivered.

The 'glass ceiling' was in evidence in the dealings with staff, as the housemaid resigned but was persuaded to stay at an increased salary of 7/- a week, whilst a new 'boy' was advertised for at 30/- a week.

In January 1916 a premium of £3 a year was approved for anti-aircraft insurance, and this was to prove foresightful in the light of what was to happen in World War II.

Some members had been drowning their sorrows, as the following excerpt indicates:

17 February 1918 – Following the reading of a letter of complaint of the shortage of whisky in the Club, it was explained that 'the difficulties under which the Club laboured owing to its having consumed half its previous years allowance (by February) and the dealers refusing to supply more. After an animated discussion it was resolved that the Secretary is to interview Burlington Stores with a view to obtaining a supply from them under a threat of transferring the Club account.

There were difficulties with the club's Steward and the situation worsened in 1919 when the Steward left under a cloud and the Secretary had to report that wines were missing.

The Skues brothers to the rescue

Whilst Mosely was keeping the NFSC going through the course of the war, the two Skues brothers successively became stand-in secretaries of the club, the younger C A M Skues until his call up for training, and G E M Skues for the rest of the war. It was noted at the AGM in June 1919 that: – "it was a remarkable fact that far from going back, the club had prospered and progressed exceedingly during the war, thanks to the efforts of those two brothers (C A M Skues and G E M Skues)." At the general committee meeting of 19th of October 1919:

"It was resolved that G E M Skues be invited to become an Honorary life Member in recognition of his great services to the Club and to angling generally."

The following year, Skues proposed in his turn that Senior should be elected an honorary member and this was approved.

An NFSC bid for post-war power foiled

At the general committee meeting of 4 March 1920 a boarding party from the NFSC was repulsed by the general committee – "

> *A letter was read from Mr A C Kent suggesting that either he or Mr Moseley should be on the General Committee as representing the sub-committee on Natural Fly Collection and the Club Journal. The Secretary was instructed to inform Mr Kent that the Committee would be very pleased by their attendance at any Committee Meeting to make any representations regarding the special honorary duties which they so kindly and effectively perform for the Club. The Committee feel that this would place them in a freer position than if they were actual members of the Committee.*"

C A N ('Tup') Wauton joined the NFSC in 1921, a well-known authority, correspondent with and supporter of Skues who was later, in 1930, to write *Trout Fisher's Entomology, An Elementary Treatise on Natural Flies*. In the FFJ in 1921 he produced an article entitled *Fly Fisher's Ephemeridae* which was also printed and sold as a handbook. This latter did not mention nymph fishing and did not describe the individual nymphs of any species, or indeed genus, all its down to earth and helpful descriptions and explanatory tables being aimed at the dry fly man alone.

Collection and imitation both thrive

In the Summer 1921, Winter 1921-22, and Autumn 1922 issues of the FFJ voluminous reports of flies collected from all over the British Isles (and abroad) were published, with enough detail on some rivers, probably, to enable useful 'then and now' comparisons. Further reports embodying manifold additions followed in the spring editions of 1925, 1926, and 1927. The NFSC was especially thanked, together with members who had been submitting specimens, by the general committee in the spring of 1923.

Also in 1921, Mosely published his book *The Dry-Fly Fisherman's Entomology*, a comprehensive and beautifully illustrated book of all the different angler's flies designed to aid identification of the hatched adult. Only two nymphs of upwinged flies were included, those of the Mayfly and the March Brown (actually that of the False March Brown). But then it is, after all, the dry fly fisherman's entomology.

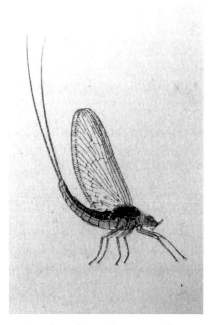

Female Medium Olive spinner from Mosely's book

Skues' time has come to imitate nymphs

This was a good time for Skues, who had published *The Way of a Trout with a Fly* in 1921. This was well received, and a second edition followed in 1928. It is a great book in my view, full of fascinating observations and imitative ideas. It is all the better because the author frequently admits to not knowing why particular patterns and presentations work. Tantalisingly, in several of these cases, in the state of our current knowledge, we should be able to enlighten him. For example, the success of a sunk red spinner puzzles him – but he, not being a wading man, had never seen a baetis spinner crawl down

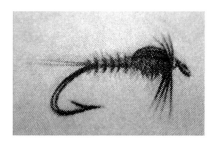

Skues' generic nymph pattern from *The Way of a Trout with a Fly*

underwater to lay its eggs. And indeed Halford had been unaware of the fact that his Detached Badger spinner imitation should properly have been fished under the surface and not as a dry fly for this very reason.

Mosely finally nails the True March Brown

The true March Brown, the fly that appears in March and April on rain-fed rivers, had been commonly confused even by the then experts with the Late, Summer, or False March Brown. It is in fact an entirely different species (*Rhithrogena germanica*, as opposed to *Ecdyonurus venosus*) and was finally identified as such in 1932 by Mosely, in its historical context which he researched comprehensively, working as Chairman of the Natural Fly Sub-Committee of the Flyfishers' Club, at the British Museum of Natural History, and as Fellow of the Royal Entomological Society. The flies that Halford listed as March Brown on the chalk streams in 1910 were all, by his own identification, *Ecdyonurus* and so False March Browns.

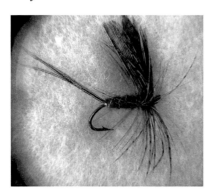

'Early March Brown, Female'
by M E Mosely
(by kind permission of Dr P Barnard)

By 1932 when Mosely wrote his March Brown identification article, exact imitation of the hatched fly in terms of identification and colour matching had more or less run its course – however leaving many other (design, constructional, and presentational) aspects unexplored, thank Heavens, to be addressed by others in the latter half of the 20th century.

Skues holds back for another 10 years

In *The Way of a Trout with a Fly*, Skues actually presented only two nymph patterns, and although it is a reasonable deduction by

70

the reader that they are generic and could be tied using materials of any colour to suit the natural, he does not really give guidance pertaining to the imitation of the larval form of any specific insect. This hesitation to give guidance on exact imitation, which amounts to pulling his punches, carried on over the next 10 years, with his publication in his writings of only a few actual imitative patterns at a time, with significant gaps in between. His last recommendation for an exact imitation had been the Iron Blue nymph in 1918, and there was a five-year gap between that and his publication of three new specifically imitative patterns in 1923; then there was a three-year gap, to 1926 when he published another four; a two-year gap to 1928 when he published three more; then another two-year gap up to 1930 (another two); and his output did not become prolific until 1931 when he produced a flurry of 11 nymph patterns. It is

clear however that during this whole period and right through to the end of his life he was constantly experimenting at the vice and sharing his ideas with his correspondents and readers.

And actually his pattern for the Iron Blue nymph is inaccurate – the natural nymph is not iron blue or anything like that colour, but various shades of olive green. We have to conclude that he did not know which nymph produced which dun.

Nymph in top right hand corner is that of the Iron Blue

Skues, inhibited, not dense

So the undertow which had had such a backwash effect upon the exact imitation of nymphs was not overcome effectively until the 1920s; and it was a series of seven waves building up to a big one that resulted rather than a tsunami. There seems, to my mind, to be no doubt that the undertow and the resultant punch-pulling by Skues resulted from his being inhibited by fears of being accused of unprincipled and ungentlemanly behaviour in fishing subsurface. He was an inspired and creative freethinker and inventor of highly effective patterns, many of them not in fact exact imitations but close caricatures of form and colour that sprang from trial and error – but worked.

The Club's Founder honoured

Getting back to the Flyfishers' Club and what was going on there, on the 20th March 1924 at the Annual General Meeting, **t**he Chairman drew the meeting's attention *"to the fact that the oldest Member of the Club, Mr. Marston was present, having been a member for 40 years; he was the only survivor of the original founders, all other members having gone to the Great Beyond."*

Last records of the NFSC

As we have seen the NFSC was extremely active under Mosely during the years up to and including 1927, but the report of that year seems to be the final report that the NFSC published in the Journal, and marks (I think) the end of its activities. Certainly, there is no reference to its activities in any surviving minute book, or in the minute books of the general committee from that point forward. However, in April 1934 a letter was received by the general committee from Mosely offering to 'make up as nearly as possible a complete collection of British caddis flies for the cabinet of pinned specimens.' His offer was gratefully accepted. We have to assume that there were still some gaps in this collection, with some of the rarer species unrepresented. The gift was presented in February 1935.

Fly-tying still central to the club, but unrecorded, or records lost

In January 1932, at the general committee, the suggestion of establishing a permanent record of well-known patterns of artificial flies was considered a good one but declined at present owning to the expense and labour involved. We might guess that this was Skues returning to his old idea – but we don't know... there had been no reference to the fly making materials sub-committee, in fact, since the 1904 annual dinner at which Skues was thanked by Halford for his work on it. In the meantime, however, over all or many of the intervening years numerous Thursday night fly-tying sessions took place at the club: these were known as the Fly-tying Scraps, and Skues was a frequent and energetic participant (there were prizes given, but Skues was not a frequent winner, being an impatient and impressionistic tyer).

In April 1920 the General Committee Minutes had recorded that:

The sum of £25 is to be made available to purchase suitable fly-dressing materials and equipment.

The NFSC, if it still remained in existence, was entirely quiescent in the 1930s.

Dry fly purism resurfaces, and Skues makes a strategic error

During the 1930s however there was a distinct recrudescence of dry fly purism with antagonism to nymph fishing gaining ground. From 1935 onwards there was a voluminous public controversy with long correspondences in *The Times*, the *Flyfishers' Journal* and the Salmon and Trout Association magazine about nymph fishing and its desirability. Skues reacted unwisely by mounting increasingly negative and eventually vitriolic attacks on Halford who of course was 20 years dead: something which did not endear the flyfishing public to him. This, together with resentment at the fact that he consistently caught more and bigger trout than they did, culminated in his being 'given the black spot' in May 1936 by the leaders of his syndicate at Abbotts Barton. One of them was Neville Bostock the shoe magnate. Bostock was the first owner of the copy of Mosely's book *The Dry-Fly Fisherman's Entomology* which I now have. In effect this was a latter-day gospel of the anti-nymphers. He was also on the Committee of the Flyfishers' Club, and no doubt had a hand in the idea of the Nymph Debate of 1938 (see below).

Nymphae non sunt muscae – nymphs are not flies

They said that his practice of using nymphs subsurface was not flyfishing, and therefore Skues had led the syndicate into a breach of the lease, which specified flyfishing only. Only dry fly fishing was flyfishing, and subsurface fishing was not. In fact he did hang on there as a member for a further two years until 1938, and did not in actual fact give up fishing the nymph, but it was not a happy time.

It got to be felt at the Flyfishers' Club that this nymphing thing was an issue that needed settling down once and for all.

Things were pretty tense generally at this time as the clouds of war gathered again, with feelings about what was and was not acceptable behaviour sharpening. As evidence I would proffer a couple of the very few 'edgy' items from the Minutes of the Committee of the club, betraying the existence of some perhaps understandably frayed tempers:

20 May 1937 – Letters dated 21st and 26th April from Mr Arthur Severn complaining of a member wearing a red tie and not wearing a hat whilst walking Piccadilly were noted. No comment was offered.

17 March 1938 – Letter of apology recorded in this Minute from Mr Carl Schelling relating to a letter from him to member Mr G. Gladwin-Errington referred by him to the General committee.

Pouring water on a drowning man

In 1938 the Great Nymph Debate took place in the club, in which Skues, although winged was not downed, and no conclusion was reached. Both sides got completely hung up on the forensic niceties of whether nymphs wriggle when rising through the water to hatch, thus missing completely the main issue. The main issue was: whether it is intelligent or not exactly to imitate the larval form of flies that fish are eating, with as much attention to detail and energy as had, following Halford, been applied to the exact imitation of hatched flies: and to fish them subsurface. An extremely comprehensive and balanced account of this debate is available in Tony Hayter's 2013 book *G E M Skues: the Man of the Nymph*. The Debate was poorly and insensitively managed, and it was not the club's finest hour. Setting Sir Joseph Ball, a hard man and a Judge at the very top of his forensic career, to make mincemeat of a man in his eighties was cruel: out of proportion to the imputed misdemeanours.

The great Nymph Debate lingers on today, interestingly, with the Piscatorial Society repeating a version of it in 2014, relative to whether their Rules should be altered to allow weighted nymphs, or remain as they are allowing only unweighted 'Skues-type' nymphs. I'm told passions were again aroused. They decided to maintain the status quo. Fair enough. But Skues used weighted nymphs beyond doubt – he just didn't dare say so.

In 1939 Skues, still kicking, presented the club with a copy of his recently published book *Nymph Fishing for Chalk Stream Trout*. And Mosely, in the same year made a gift to the club of 40 bottles of different coloured dyes for dying feathers. But after many years of friendly correspondence with Skues, usually also involving John Evans, Mosely had joined the anti-Skues camp together with Sir Joseph Ball, Halford's scary High Court Judge posthumous defense counsel in the Debate, and they both wrote scathing reviews of his new book, in contrast with the good reception it had received from other pundits, each returning to the rather meaningless issue of whether rising nymphs wriggle or are inert.

Mosely and Skues retreat, each to his refuge

History now forced these two brilliant men to live in parallel universes, unable to get on with each other and not communicating except to criticise. Mosely, who said to their mutual correspondent

Monkhouse "that he was not in the least interested in nymphs and anybody who fished the nymph was in his opinion a bad thing" – not exactly the point of view one would expect from an enquiringly-minded scientist – was writing determinedly learned scientific papers from a taxonomic point of view, mainly on the Trichoptera, from his adopted base at the British Museum of Natural History. Skues was corresponding, from his new and rather sad home in Wiltshire, with anyone and everyone who was interested in trout behaviour and the design and construction of trout flies whether dry or wet, and blaming the dry fly purists (not wrongly) for his effective expulsion from Abbots Barton. By 1947 he had 'through age and infirmity' given all his fly-dressing materials (three large Elephant files) to the Flyfishers' Club and given up tying flies. Mosely was not much in the Flyfishers' Club, and Skues not at all.

The two genetic strains of flyfishing personality, twin helixes but twining in opposite directions like the columbine and the bindweed, having briefly intertwined now once again diverged, to the detriment of the sport and of the successful imitation of fly – and they were now to stay apart until the deaths of these two survivors of each.

What might have been – the wasted years

Just think what might have resulted if they could together have applied their brilliant minds and penetrating powers of observation to the actual behaviour of nymphs rising to hatch. We now know that nymphs do wriggle as they rise through the water column, but become inert to the human eye on making contact with the underside of the meniscus, their hydrophobic wing covers breaking through it, splitting it apart, and their hydrophilic shuck gripping it at the edge so that the wings, thorax, abdomen and legs can sequentially emerge with the legs pushing against the held shuck. Perceptive observers like Stuart Crofts have both described how it works and disseminated the information widely through flyfishing circles. Halford himself had aquaria and sinks, and must have watched it happen thousands of times – so indeed had Mosely at the BMNH, and we can be 100% certain that both had watched nymphs rise and hatch.

Mosley was in fact a brilliant taxonomist but perhaps less good a behaviouralist: for example, as late as 1940 he published in the *Flyfishers' Club Journal* a paper making out that the Ephemerid nymph was akin to the larval cockroach and could only achieve separation between its outer skin and its inner, sub-imago's epidermis by pausing long enough at the surface film to suck air and inflate itself. His colleague Kimmins quickly put him right on that by showing that the nymphs of many species acquire intradermal gas without visiting the surface. This may at the least be indicative of a lesser interest on Mosely's part, in the behavioural side of larval stages. Indeed, there's no evidence of any great interest on the part of either man, in the identification of the larval stages.

Nymph-ism (i.e. as in age-ism, sex-ism)

Through the operations of the NFSC, Halford and Mosely had hundreds of anglers spend tens of thousands of hours all over the country, collecting and posting to London tens of thousands of

specimens for identification and for assessment as to the possibility and value of imitating them. But as far as we can tell, scarcely a single one of these specimens was a nymph (a single caddis larva, *Hydropsyche* species was sent in from the Windrush in 1927 – the exception proving the rule).

It was not until the middle 1900s that a major effort was made to identify nymphs as being the larval forms of specific species. When Peter Barnard told me this, I was surprised. He says that it was just very much easier to identify the adult, and that is therefore how it was done – and this I can understand in terms of what you might ask keen anglers to do and report on. But it is a bit puzzling for the scientist: nymphs are hundreds of times more plentiful than adults, and easier to catch; they can easily be held in a tank to see what they hatch into, and the nymph's identifying features 'reverse-engineered' from there. There seems to have been no curiosity to do so, and I'm afraid I'm led to think that, once again, the reason for this was distaste, of a moral kind, on the part of the natural fly show ringmasters.

Emerger-ism

And neither Halford, nor Mosely, in spite of seeing so many flies hatch in the wild and in aquaria and hence being very familiar with the process of emergence, could bring themselves to concede that the emerger was worth imitating; so they never referred to it as a separate stage. The former admitted that trout could be 'bulging' to nymphs under the surface, but never really spoke or wrote about trout taking emergers. (Skues did, and wrote clearly in *The Way of a Trout with a Fly* that to the trout seeking to conserve energy and gain maximum food value, emergers were a sitting duck target). Mosely was the most advanced natural fly expert of his age who was also an advanced angler and a keen fly tyer. And yet if you look in his book *The Dry-Fly Fisherman's Entomology* (1921), you will find no reference to emerging, or emergers, or eclosion, or ecdusis. You will find in the first chapter, on capturing specimens, no reference to a subsurface net, to nymphs, or to emerging flies. He recommends catching specimen duns, when sitting on the surface, on your landing net handle, in backwaters. Dr Peter Barnard defends these omissions, referring to the title of the book: *The Dry-Fly Fisherman's Entomology*; a good point, but I think we could have expected the angler to have been given more help to understand what goes on at the water's surface, by someone who, after all, did know.

Both camps to blame

For the last 50 years how to succeed in imitating the emerger has been the hottest topic in flyfishing the world over. The emergence of the topic of emergers was delayed, pushed back down below the surface as it were by Halford, and then kept as far as ever possible in limbo by Mosely, between them for – well, shall we say sixty years?

And did Skues really help? The honest answer has to be, no, not really. He pulled his punches inhibitedly for thirty years until 1921, producing virtually no nymph patterns that looked like one, quietly practising what

Skues going fishing,
E A Barton's sketch

he didn't dare to preach in terms of proper imitation of the nymph until then.

He did really get going with nymph imitation during the 1920s and was in the process of converting the majority of fly fishermen across the country, but as the 1930s progressed he threw the baby out with the bathwater by returning unnecessarily to the attack on Halford. Halford had been dead for twenty years, for Heavens sake. Hero Skues may be, and he is mine, but he had largely himself to blame for his troubles, including his effective expulsion from the Itchen and the Great Nymph Debate. He saw himself as in the right in logic, and the Halfordians saw themselves as in the right in moral terms.

The wasted hatches

His fault or Halford's? Does it really matter? Together they made an absolute Horlicks of it.

And the really wasteful thing about the Horlicks they made; of what might have been 60 years of superb innovation and achievement in flyfishing, is: a) that they screwed it up for everybody and not just for themselves – and b) worst of all, they crippled the development of fully imitative flyfishing over a period co-extensive with the last six decades of good fly hatches.

Other imitative developments of the first half of the 20th century

The Flyfishers' Club was the greatest single hub of imitative development during the period that followed Halford's (including of course Marryatt's) excellent general precepts on how best to create and present the fly imitatively (dry only please); and it was still the hub during the later period that bracketed Skues' slow revealing of his thinking and practise. Within the club, J C Mottram did arguably better work on the imitation of nymphs than Skues, and published it much earlier, with very specific instructions as to how both resting and swimming nymphs should be fished, in *Fly-Fishing: Some New Arts and Mysteries*, in 1915 – but he, like C E Walker, was rather swamped in terms of how much notice people took, by Halford and all his works. Later, he recanted and dished the dirt on Skues in the Great Debate: something that was out of kilter with his position as a scientist, still defies rational explanation, and after which he rather slunk away. In 1924 came the groundbreaking new book *Sunshine and the Dry Fly* by J W Dunne: still a work that makes you think, even though the recipe flies faded from use fairly quickly. Then in 1931 Col E W Harding, another club member, published his scientifically based analysis of how trout see the fly and the fisherman: *The Flyfisher & the Trout's Point of View*, which embraced the nymph as much as the dry fly with, amongst several others, a superb colour plate of how nymphs are progressively more clearly seen by the fish – and they look like the real thing. (I am lucky enough to have the Colonel's own copy, with extensive notes for a second edition that never came to pass). Meanwhile other, photographic, work was being published on how fish see things under water and above it by Dr Francis Ward: *Marvels of Fish Life as Revealed by the Camera* in 1911 and *Animal Life Under Water* in 1919 – works with which Skues and Harding were both familiar.

Edmonds and Lee, and Lunn

Probably the two greatest contributions to the angler's ability to match the natural fly that were made in this period, beyond those of Halford and Skues themselves, came from outside the club. Firstly, Edmonds and Lee in *Brook and River Trouting*, published in 1916, made a wonderful job of showing how to imitate, with artificials both dry and wet, the flies of the Yorkshire rivers. Secondly, William Lunn created a total of 40 patterns in effective imitation

Lunn inspecting natural fly

of the flies of the chalk streams: whilst he was not a member himself, what was effectively his book, *River Keeper* (1934) was encouraged by his boss at Houghton on the Test, A N Gilbey, and written by J W Hills the well-known author of *A Summer on the Test* (both of whom were members of the club). Lunn's work was extraordinary, as he had been born in poor circumstances, worked from the age of seven, and taught himself aquatic entomology and fly-dressing during 50 years of working as head keeper at Houghton on the Test. His 'Lunn's Particular' is one of the best-known and most successful imitations of the Baetis spinner of all time. It was designed to fish in the film, and its creator was perhaps the first person at the centre of flyfishing development to have observed that the Baetis spinners crawl down under water to lay their eggs and float up to the underside of the surface when spent rather than falling onto it from above. Two successive anecdotal passages in Chapter 13 of *River Keeper* make his realisation of this fact, and his strategy to exploit it with the Lunn's Particular, quite clear. Only the entomologist A E Eaton is known to have noticed this behaviour earlier.

A N Gilbey & Wm Lunn with a stock fish

C A N Wauton in his overview booklet *Fly-fisher's Ephemeridae* of 1921 is clearly unaware of Baetis crawl-down.

Lunn had made himself into a scientist and conducted many long-running surveys of fly hatches and fly behaviour, as well as numerous experiments. He was responsible after long persistence, in reintroducing mayfly to the river, originating the suspended glass plate technique that is still used today, although he himself in the end doubted whether his work had been the key factor. 27 of

Lunn's exemplar Particular from the Flyfishers Club Collection

Lunn's patterns, tied by him, are on display at the Flyfishers' Club. I myself own an example of the Lunn's Particular, bought at one of the 1980s rummage sales of the club amongst what was then viewed as miscellaneous rubbish: the provenance was a club member B J C Spurway and it lives in a State Express 555 cigarette box in a bit of hollowed out expanded polystyrene ceiling tile covered with Sellotape together with a companion in not quite such a good state, with an accompanying folded piece of paper on which is written 'The First Lunn's Particular, tied in 1917. Presented by B J C Spurway.' I have no idea whether it is the original, but I like to think it may be.

Dr H A Bell, and R C Bridgett

In the early years of the 20th century lake fishing gained popularity, in particular with the opening of the first drinking water reservoirs. Blagdon was the earliest and most famous of these, opened in 1903, stocked with brown trout and opened for fishing in 1904. J C Mottram fished there in the early years, and, noticing the rather different fly-life (dominantly buzzers and Corixae) set out to imitate it. Amongst other patterns, he originated a buzzer imitation tied right round the bend of the hook with alternating white and black bands – the same as many years later became the 'Footballer' of Geoffrey Bucknall. We can surmise that this work was being undertaken in the 10 years prior to the publication of Mottram's first book in 1915. The tradition of non-Ephemeropteran imitation, which had been started by C E Walker in 1898 but been steamrollered by the dry fly revolution, was

Dr HA Bell serving in the Home Guard

kept going in this way by Mottram. Not too long afterwards Dr Howard Bell bought the doctor's practice at Wrington close to the reservoir following a bad war experience and started fishing Blagdon every week – and did so for nearly half a century. He seems to have fished there from 1920, and although his work is almost entirely unpublished because of his modesty and hatred of publicity of any kind, he progressively invented eight or ten new patterns imitative of Blagdon's fly life, some of which like his black buzzer and amber nymph are still in successful use today. The Amber Nymph imitates the 'pharate adult', swim-up stage of a locally-common caddis which he used to find crawling up his waders. Dr Bell's other contribution was in terms of presentation – he insisted that his patterns should be fished "maddeningly slowly" like the naturals.

In Scotland R C Bridgett was also working on imitations of the natural flies of the lochs during the early 1920s, and in 1924 he published a collection of articles he wrote for the Glasgow Herald newspaper in the form of the book *Loch Fishing In Theory and Practice*. His particular imitations were of upwing nymphs, buzzers, and sedges as well as the shrimp. These two lake fishing imitators of the natural fly, Bell and Bridgett, are the progenitors of the stillwater revolution which got going after the Second World War, and has now overtaken river fishing in terms of the number of anglers involved: and although in the first few decades of that there was a steady progression away from imitation of the natural flies, the process has reversed in recent years.

Cosmo Barrett

A great deal of creative work was going on outside of the Flyfishers' Club ambit in the first half of the 20th century, and it is an area of study that would repay time spent. For present purposes I can only really pick out these few of the most important developers: but amongst them I must include Cosmo Barrett who moved to Presteigne in Wales with his brother in 1928, setting up shop to build rods and tie flies. He invented (or rather re-invented since it had been first proposed by Alexander Mackintosh in *The Driffield Angler* in

1806) the reverse-tied dry fly with the hackle at the bend, in the shape of the Barrett's Bane and the Barrett's Professor – a forerunner of the Leckford Professor, probably. He and the Welsh author James Evans liked them because they floated better, hooked better, and the hackle stayed cleaner. I like them because when the wind is in the face of an upstream dry fly fisherman, they face the same way as the newly hatched dun, i.e. into the wind. Hardy Brothers stole and marketed the patterns in fact, and Barrett forced them to settle out of court.

World War II heroic actions

Returning to our timeline, in 1939 World War II was declared. Skues thought seriously of giving up fishing for the duration, as being just plain inappropriate. In August 1940 44 yards of blackout curtain was delivered to the club, and on 7th of November 1940 a brief minute of the general committee recorded the partial demolition by enemy action on 13th October of the top two floors of the club premises in Piccadilly. The club president himself, Charles Giveen, who had been dining at the club with one companion when a shower of incendiaries fell, saved the entirety of the club and its collections by putting an incendiary bomb in a bucket of sand and carrying it together with the Steward from where it had fallen into a top storey room, out into the street. Then, as flames swept in from neighbouring premises, he organised a hosepipe from a bathroom tap and together with the Steward and two passing soldiers spent several exhausting hours running from one fire to another on different floors putting them out. (The full story is told in Tony Hayter's book *G E M Skues: The Man of the Nymph*, 2013, pp 298-9).

Almost destroyed

Members defiantly carried on using the club under a tarpaulin roof for several more months, until on the 16th of April 1941 a landmine exploded in the street, and the building was declared unsafe. Four days were allowed to remove the club's possessions to various places of greater safety and the members were welcomed to a refuge by the Garrick Club. On 21 April 1941 an emergency general committee meeting recorded that the premises had been seriously damaged by enemy action, and the remaining possessions of the club were sent away for storage and restoration as appropriate. This was when the pinned and fluid collections were blown about and the third cabinet was irretrievably damaged (see Appendices 2 and 3).

In September 1941, *'a motion that the Club be put into cold storage for the remainder of the War was negatived'*.

Without in any way belittling the suffering, heroism, and hardiness of all concerned in the war, the attitude was largely business as usual, 'carry on and have a cup of tea', for club members for the rest of the duration except of course for many members being lost through resignations and deaths, and for a certain amount of further bomb damage to the library whilst in storage. And they no longer had access to the key resources of the club, the library, the collections or the singular companionship of other fly fishermen. Probably very little thought was devoted to exact imitation. Any flyfishing was welcomed, but as a break from the grinding realities of life. As the war neared its end, Coopers set about repairing the cased fish, others the pictures, and happily for everybody 197 bottles of

THE DUFFER—THE MAN WITHOUT SKILL OF HAND, WITHOUT

vintage port stored in Didcot for safekeeping were returned to the club. Skues was formally thanked for being such a generous benefactor to the damaged club Library having presented nearly 100 volumes. A few of these were sold by the club recently, and I was very happy indeed to acquire Skues' own inscribed copy of *Fly-Fishing for Duffers* by R D Peck (1934), illustrated by the famous cartoonist and keen angler H M Bateman (left).

The nymph business still exhibited a nasty little half-life, though:

12 October 1944 - Correspondence between Major Deller and Mr G E M Skues was considered, the former representing that 'nymphs' should be restricted to certain dressings only. The Committee concurred with Mr Skues view that the suggestion was neither practical nor desirable and agreed that, in any case, it was not within the province of the Club to attempt to make or enforce such restriction.

You would think that the fifth year of war would have returned that tiny issue to its proper perspective, but no, there were still some pretty sad people sniping away at the 85-year-old.

Twin silos still standing

Both men died in successive Augusts after the War – Mosely in 1948 and Skues in 1949.

The separate silos of operation that each of them set up in the Flyfishers' Club (Halford's and Mosely's Natural Fly Sub-Committee: and Skues' fly-dressing materials committee) each with their commodious cabinets and collections, had stayed more or less separate silos through the whole of the first half of the twentieth century. Post WWII, virtually nothing was done with either of them for another sixty years until the new millennium, and the development of imitative fly-dressing has almost entirely taken place elsewhere than actually in the premises of (and has not been particularly encouraged by or moderated by) the London Flyfishers' Club over that period. In the Fourth Age of Flyfishing, Post World War 2, the club has not itself been the spur to development that it was in the Third Age.

Prejudice persists post-War

Prejudice against nymphing formed an enduring environment for the young flyfisher after the War, including of course our own Boomer generation. If you ask what was the most influential fishing book for

SPRING

These are the flies that Mr. Crabtree uses

| Blue Dun | Olive Dun | Greenwell's Glory | Gold-ribbed Hare's Ear | Iron Blue Dun | Ginger Quill | Orange Quill | Red Quill |

The Blue Dun is an imitation of the earliest natural fly of the fisherman's season. The Olive Dun is an imitation of the natural fly of that name and can be used all through the season. Greenwell's Glory is one of the best suggestions of several of the Ephemeridæ ever invented. It is good all through the season. Gold-ribbed Hare's Ear also suggests several natural flies and is an all-round-the-season fly. The Iron Blue Dun imitates the natural fly of that name, and when the fish are taking it, it is a deadly fly. The Ginger Quill is a general fly which particularly suggests the Pale Watery Dun. The Orange Quill is a very valuable fly when trout are feeding on the Blue Winged Olive. The Red Quill is a good general fly which will take trout that are feeding on olives. It is known as the "Dry fly man's sheet anchor on a strange river."

| Olive Horse Hair | Blue Horse Hair | Red Tag | Wickham's Fancy | Caperer | Grannom | Silver Sedge | Medium Sedge |

Here are two flies which Mr. Crabtree tied himself. The first one has a body of white horsehair over a hook shank painted a strong olive colour which shows through the horse hair. The second one has the horse hair over a blue shank. He has found both very successful. The Red Tag is a good fancy fly, particularly for grayling. Wickham's Fancy is another very good fancy fly that is sometimes deadly. This pattern called the Caperer was invented by the Late W. J. Lunn and is a very good fly indeed under many different conditions. The Grannom is an imitation of the natural sedge fly of that name that comes in April, and is the earliest of the sedges. The rest of the sedge flies appear from May onwards. There are many of them, but two or three artificial patterns will imitate most of them. Here are two reliable patterns to use through the season.

| Cocky-bondhu | Soldier Palmer | Mr. Crabtree's Mayfly | Mayfly | Mr. Crabtree's Mayfly Spinner (spent snail) | March Brown | Tup's Indispensable | Alder |

The Cocky-bondhu imitates a beetle but it is a good general fly to use at all times. The Soldier Palmer is a fancy fly that will often take trout on rocky rivers. It is also a very good fly for chub if used in a large size, say 3 or 4 or even larger. There is no end to the patterns of the Mayfly. Those shown are good. The first one is one tied by Mr. Crabtree. In general the hackle patterns are very much better than those with wings. This is also the case with other flies, though not so much as with mayflies. The March Brown imitates the natural fly of the same name, and is good all round the season on rocky streams. Tup's Indispensable is an excellent general fly which imitates several spinners. The Alder is a very good fly when the natural Alder is on the water, but it will also take fish at many other times, even when the Mayfly is on.

47

all of us, the answer is *Mr Crabtree Goes Fishing* by Bernard Venables, published in 1949 and my own bible during my formative years as an angler. No other book came near its influence on young minds. In it, all of Mr Crabtree's 24 recommended flies for trout and chub (above) are without exception dry, and there's no mention at all of emergers, whilst nymphs are only mentioned as the immature stage before the fly hatches. The author does mention in passing that trout eat more nymphs than hatched duns, but nymph imitation is not mentioned.

The expatriation of imitation

There has indeed been a huge growth in flyfishing thought, experimentation and innovation over these last 60 years. Most of that has been directed at the successful imitation of subsurface trout food items and of emergers. Although a fair amount of it has taken place in the UK with writers such as Clarke, Edwards, Goddard, Patterson, and Sawyer, the UK has not really been the dominant home of imitative flyfishing innovation, and it would be fair to say that the greater bulk of the activity has taken place in the USA, with the field being led by writers like Cutter, Harrop, Harvey, Lafontaine, Marinaro, Proper, Schullery, Swisher & Richards, and Wright.

Reculer pour mieux sauter

That said, the Flyfishers' Club is now far from being in a state of suspended animation. As David Beazley, the Librarian, has recently pointed out, 18 author members have produced over three dozen titles in the last 13 years, and much of the research for these books has been enabled by the club, and carried out in it. Indeed the club has immensely strengthened and organised its historical records, its collections, its memorabilia, and its library in the last dozen years – and now represents one of the, perhaps the, greatest single resource and repository of flyfishing information (including the best natural fly reference collections) worldwide. In the Fourth Age of Flyfishing, the club is ... poised.

Fin – or rather tail-piece

From 1800 to 1950, the Imitators of the Fly forged much of flyfishing as we know it, their work springing from a melting pot of contributory influences and resources. The country hit an economic sweet spot, and a wealthy aspirational middle-class emerged whose one great desire was to be a gentleman. Mass production, mass marketing, and speedy delivery of flyfishing tackle had arrived. Travel to rivers was easy. Authorities were in the process of carving out their niches; their written works published not just in book form but in responsive media which were as extensive and detailed as today's blogs, forums, and websites. Personalities clashed however, and the fullest development of imitation was hamstrung during the golden years of natural fly hatches.

A footnote on Alfred Ronalds' book
The Fly-Fisher's Entomology 1836

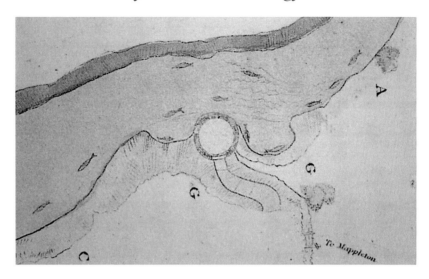

On page five of Ronald's book, Plate One exhibits what I think is another first in flyfishing literature in the shape of a diagram of the River Blithe showing with little trout drawings the likely location of fish in relation to the lay of the banks and the current, rocks, shoals, 'scours' (riffles), and eddies. I don't remember seeing a mention of this elsewhere, but it also shows his brushwood-constructed observation hut, as in the magnified picture above. He describes it as having three windows, one looking out over a scour which you can see to the right of the hut, the top of the riffle therefore being right in front of the outward looking window; and the other two windows each looking sideways into an eddy. He had heaped up earth banks on either side of the inward path so that the observer could gain access without scaring fish: and he had fitted curtains to the windows so that he could observe fish without being seen. His observations of the reactions of trout and grayling to the fly were not confined to this location, as he fished all over Derbyshire and Staffordshire, but many of his experiments were carried out here (for example feeding pepper and mustard coated houseflies to fish to see if they would reject them or spit them out – they didn't).

Appendix 1 : What flies were found where

fly never walked down a window-pane that was absolutely clean, and he could not walk down the side of a milk-bowl because it was greasy. It was nothing of a joke when he fell in, for doctors had declared that the cause of the death of so many young children in the summer was their drinking milk in which flies, after eating contaminated matter, had been drowned. The buzzing of flies, the lecturer said, was not properly understood. It was thought to be due to the movements of the wings, but the buzzing would go on if the wings were removed, and a more reasonable view was that it was due to the passage of air through the tubes of the body.

[It seems incredible that Mr. H. Hill should believe the buzzing noise made by flies is made by "the passage of air through their bodies." It is surely purely vibration from the wings.—ED. F. G.]

Fish Culture

THE following note is from the famous Howietoun Fishery, Stirling :—

"The spawning season here has been protracted owing to hard frosts, the ponds having been again and again covered with ice up to five inches thick. This, of course, retarded the fish from spawning, and entailed extra hard work; but the weather is milder now, and the spawning season will soon be finished. The quality of the ova is excellent, and there are now over three million trout eggs lying on the grilles, and about a quarter of a million already sent off, some of them now on their way to India. As you may be aware, all our stock-fish breeders are fed on natural food, principally shellfish, and so the ova is all of the very best quality."

Natural Fly Collection

IN publishing these first tables of a systematic and scientific classification of the trout-fisher's entomology, the Natural Fly Committee of the Fly Fishers' Club tender their sincere thanks to all those members of the angling public who have so kindly assisted in the work of collecting. All specimens received are being carefully tabulated, as will be seen by the tables below, and as soon as sufficiently complete information is collected, tables relating to other rivers are to be published.

The Natural Fly Committee would point out that the flies on the River Test may be accepted as flies likely to be found on other South of England chalk-streams, their observations up to the present showing that the flies on the following rivers are :—

River Itchen .. Same flies as River Test, with addition of Nos. 3 and 4 during May and June.

Anton .. Same flies as River Test, with the exception of Nos. 1 to 6 (May Flies).

Wiley .. Same flies as River Test. (It is stated, however, that May Flies have been found in considerable numbers in this river later than June, and a fair hatch has been seen in Oct.)

Kennet .. Same flies as River Test, with addition of Nos. 3 and 4 during May and June, a large Stone Fly during April and May; also a heavy hatch of Grannom, No. 29, in mid-April in the Newbury district. (Mr. F. M. Halford reported that in 1893-96, when fishing this river at Ramsbury, the blue-winged Olives, No. 22 and 23, were often present in the spring, even as early as April.)

FREDERIC M. HALFORD,
Chairman of the Natural Fly Committee of the Fly Fishers' Club.

FLIES FOUND ON THE RIVER TEST.

(The Numbers refer to the flies in the List of Flies.)

March .. .. 7, 8, 9, 10.
April .. .. 7, 8, 9, 10, 11, 12, 13, 18, 19, 20, 21, 26, 27, 46.
May .. .. 1, 2, 5, 6, 7, 8, 9, 10, 11, 12, 13, 14, 15, 16, 17, 18, 19, 20, 21, 29, 30, 34, 35, 36, 37, 43, 46, 50.
June .. .. 1, 2, 5, 6, 7, 8, 9, 10, 11, 12, 13, 14, 15, 16, 17, 18, 19, 20, 21, 22, 23, 24, 25, 26, 27, 29, 30, 34, 35, 36, 37, 38, 40, 41, 42, 43, 44, 45, 46, 50.
July .. .. 7, 8, 11, 12, 13, 14, 15, 16, 17, 18, 19, 20, 21, 22, 23, 24, 25, 26, 27, 28, 34, 35, 36, 38, 39, 40, 41, 42, 44, 46.
August .. .. 7, 8, 11, 12, 13, 14, 15, 16, 17, 18, 19, 20, 21, 22, 23, 24, 25, 26, 27, 28, 34, 35, 36, 38, 40, 41, 42, 44, 46.
September .. 7, 8, 11, 12, 13, 14, 15, 16, 17, 18, 19, 20, 21, 22, 23, 24, 25, 26, 27, 28, 34, 38, 40, 41, 42, 44, 46, 47.

October .. .. 7, 8, 9, 10, 11, 12, 13, 14, 15, 16, 17, 18, 19, 20, 21, 22, 23, 24, 25, 26, 27, 34, 40, 41, 42, 44, 46, 47.
November .. 9, 10, 11, 12, 18, 19, 20, 21, 42, 47, 55.
December .. 9, 10, 11, 12.

* FLIES FOUND ON THE RIVER WHARFE (YORKSHIRE).

March ..
April .. .. 7.
May .. .. 7, 14, 18, 38, 48.
June .. .. 1, 14, 18, 29, 38, 46, 48, 49, 50, 51.
July .. .. 18, 22, 29, 36, 37, 38, 48, 49, 50, 51, 52.
August .. .. 14, 18, 22, 36, 48, 49, 50, 53, 54.
September ..
October ..
November ..
December ..

* NOTE.—Flies from the River Wharfe were kindly collected by Messrs. Norman N. Lee, A. H. Illingworth, W. G. Bainbridge, and Dr. Hoyle.

LIST OF FLIES.

No.	Name	Sex	Species
1.	May Fly—Green	Male	Ephemera danica.
2.	" "	Female	
3.	" Brown "	Male	Ephemera vulgata or E. lineata.
4.	" " "	Female	
5.	Spent Gnat	Male	Ephemera danica, vulgata, or lineata.
6.	" "	Female	
7.	Olive Dun	Male	
8.	" "	Female	Baëtis vernus or B. rhodani.
9.	Dark Olive Dun	Male	
10.	" " "	Female	
11.	Olive Spinner	Male	
12.	" "	Female	
13.	" (red)	Female	
14.	Pale Watery Dun	Male	
15.	" " "	Female	Baëtis binoculatus, Centroptilum luteolum, or Centroptilum pennulatum.
16.	Pale Watery Spinner	Male	
17.	" " "	Female	
18.	Iron Blue Dun	Male	
19.	" " "	Female	
20.	" Spinner	Male (Jenny Spinner)	Baëtis pumilus.
21.	" "	Female	
22.	Blue-winged Olive	Male	
23.	" "	Female	
24.	Sherry Spinner	Male	Ephemerella ignita.
25.	" "	Female	
26.	Black Gnat	Male	Bibio johannis.
27.	" "	Female	
28.	Brown Ant	—	
29.	Welshman's Button	Male	Sericostoma personatum.
30.	" "	Female	
31.	Small Dark Sedge	—	
32.	Medium Sedge	—	NOTE.—These three patterns of artificial flies are suggested as representing many of the Sedges, and should suffice for Sedge fishing in most chalk-streams.
33.	Cinnamon Sedge	—	
34.	Fisherman's Curse	—	Hilara obscura, various species of Simulium, etc.
35.	Brown Silverhorns	—	Leptocerus cinereus.
36.	Black "	—	Mystacides nigra, azurea, and some species of Leptocerus.
37.	Alder	—	Sialis lutaria.
38.	Yellow May Dun and Spinner	—	Heptagenia sulphurea.
39.	Grannom	—	Brachycentrus subnubilus.
40.	A Sedge represented by No. 31	Male	Goëra pilosa.
41.	" " No. 32	Female	
42.	A Cinnamon Sedge, represented by No. 33	—	Limnophilus lunatus.
43.	Large Red Sedge	—	Phryganea grandis; Phryganea striata.
44.	Caperer	—	Halesus radiatus; Halesus digitatus.
45.	Grey Sedge	—	Odontocerum albicorne.
46.	A Cinnamon Sedge, represented by No. 32	—	Rhyacophila dorsalis.
47.	Willow Fly	—	Leuctra geniculata.
48.	Stone Fly (small species)	—	Nemoura cinerea; Nemoura meyeri.
49.	March Brown	—	Ecdyurus venosus; Ecdyurus insignis; Ecdyurus volitans; Ecdyurus lateralis.
50.	Yellow Sally	—	Isopteryx torrentium; Chloroperla grammatica.
51.	This species of Dun has no popular name, but resembles a large pale Olive Dun	—	Rithrogenia semicolorata.
52.	Very small dark Sedge	—	
53.	Very small light reddish Sedge	—	Polycentropus flavomaculatus.
54.	Dark Sedge, represented by No. 31	—	Tinodes waeneri.
55.	Dark Sedge, represented by No. 31	—	Drusus annulatus.
			Chaetopteryx villosa.

NOTE.—The above numbers from 1 to 30 correspond with those of the Halford Series of new patterns, which should suffice for fishing the majority of chalk-streams.

Appendix 2 : The evidence for the three cabinets housing the Natural Fly Collections

There were three main, large cabinets, each the same as the two extant ones. Two of them contained exemplars preserved in formalin in 'watch glasses', with 18 tray drawers each containing 18 glass blocks. One of these fluid collections presented the Upwings, the Stoneflies and miscellaneous other imitatable trout food items, and the other was dedicated to Mosely's Sedges .

The evidence for the third cabinet is this:

In March 1910, Mr Gathorne Hardy joined the NFSC, and the minutes make it clear that a sum of £20 that was approved included funding for a 'third cabinet'. This finally confirms our belief that there was a third one. Mosely's article in the first ever issue of the *Flyfishers' Journal* in April 1911, reporting the work of the NFSC refers to only two cabinets so far in existence – one fluid, and one pinned and dried, and the latter of sedges only. But in his further article in the *Flyfishers' Journal* number 3 January 1912 he reported that the new, and third cabinet had been placed in the club, and said it "will be reserved entirely for the sedges, which greatly outnumber in variety of species the duns, stone flies, and other water flies familiar to the fishermen. The flies will all be mounted in 'solid watch glasses' filled with formalin. It is hoped in time to place two complete collections of the sedges in the club, one pinned, set out, and dried, the other in fluid. The old Cabinet will be reserved for the Ephemeridae, Sialidae (the alder), Perlidae (the stone flies), the Diptera, and such other insects and objects as are of interest to the trout fisher, the flyfisher in particular." This paragraph at last provides the clarity that we have been looking for. I believe it is the only source that does.

We can be pretty certain that the 'old Cabinet' referred to by Mosely here, with an engraved plate thanking Mr Harry Mear who funded it in 1900 (this is, crucially, not present on the surviving cabinet) was irretrievably damaged by the 'Hun Bomb' on 16th April 1941 – and the contents transferred to the currently existing fluid

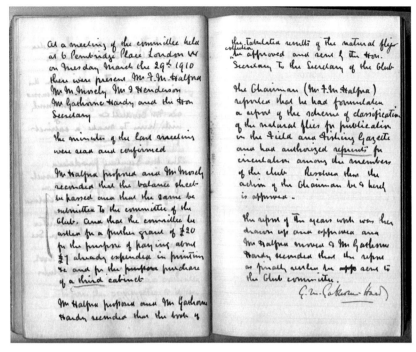

Evidence for the third cabinet, and for the Tabulation having been completed

cabinet (probably itself damaged – and there is evidence of drawers being modified to fit it); with Mosely rescuing his sedge collection out of that cabinet to the British Museum of Natural History where he worked. (We cannot be absolutely certain of all this forensic evidence and detective work, but Mosely's FFJ January 1912 article seems conclusive when taken together with the non-survival of a cabinet bearing the Mears memorial plate).

Collection and identification of the sedges was Mosely's very special interest, and we know that he had amassed a collection amounting to thousands of them even before he joined the NFSC. It is a pretty safe bet that he continued to fill this new, third, fluid cabinet with Trichoptera between the FFJ article date of 1912, and 1941 the date of the 'Hun Bomb'. In passing, we should note that Mosely must, by 1912, have once again been able to source watch glasses, probably from a resurrected Taylor & Sons.

The two surviving natural fly cabinets flanking the fur and feather cabinet.

Incidentally, there is firm evidence that after Halford died in March 1914, his main collection of specimens in fluid, the personal collection that he did not donate to the Flyfishers' Club, was taken over by Mosely, and housed by him either at his home, or at the BMNH. In January 1932, in *The Annals and Magazine of Natural History* Series 10, vol ix p 91, Mosely in his important article on the final identification of the true March Brown as *Rhithrogena haarupi* (now *germanica*) refers to making a search in "the late F M Halford's collection which is in my possession." He also searched through "the mass of material sent me by angling correspondents over a period of more than twenty years" (i.e. since he took over as Chairman of the Natural Fly Sub Committee) which makes it clear that he was the keeper of all the exemplars sent in by club members and others during that long and productive period of NFSC-inspired collection. What happened to all that vast number of examples? We don't know, but it seems likely that what he had at home became 'house clearance' on his own death in 1948, since he had no heirs. We know that the Natural History Museum (as it now is) quite recently threw away his collection of artificials, although a small number were saved at the time of this, shall we say, 'non-consultative disposal.'

Appendix 3 : What flies got blown up?

A baker's dozen species of upwing fly that are of particular imitative importance to the fly angler were lost when the Mears Cabinet was blown up. The other specimens that that cabinet contained were fairly certainly transferred to the third cabinet which had until then housed the work-in-progress fluid collection of caddisflies that Mosely was building (with him probably moving that later collection to the BMNH). We can assume that the lost specimens had to be thrown away because the tops of their watch glasses were broken. The project current at the time of writing involves replacing these exemplars with new ones, Dr Cyril Bennett breeding them through and temporarily preserving them after photographing them, and Dr Peter Barnard permanently preserving them in new watch glasses using propylene phenoxetol.

The collection still contains, largely in a pristine state and undamaged, good samples of all the rarer and less 'useful' upwings; the stoneflies, such that are important as trout food; the main caddis flies that anglers meaningfully imitate; the Diptera such as the Hawthorn fly and the Chironomids; and several other airborne and waterborne trout foods such as the Alder fly and the *Corixa*.

The flies that have been lost

1) The Medium Olive. *Baetis vernus.*
Probably the most-noticed and hence the most imitated of all the river flies. Hence frequently referred to as the 'sheet anchor' of the fly fisherman. The plan is to insert new examples of the nymph, the dun in both sexes, and the spinner in both sexes. Although common on the chalk streams, its distribution elsewhere is somewhat limited. In its place on rain fed rivers and elsewhere in the country is the somewhat bigger Large Dark Olive, which we do have good examples of in the collection.

2) The Mayfly. *Ephemera danica.*
This very important imitative target in its season in May and June is easily recognised and perhaps more easily imitated – or perhaps the fish just go crazy for it. The plan is to insert new examples of the nymph, the dun in both sexes, and the spinner in both sexes.

3) The Olive Upright. *Rhithrogena semicolorata.*
This abundant and widespread fly is one that demands the angler's attention all over the UK. The plan is to insert new examples of the nymph, and the spinner in both sexes.

4) The Large Spurwing. *Centroptilum pennulatum.*
This is now quite a rare fly but it has one distinguishing characteristic that makes it easier to imitate in that it rides down the stream with its wings parted unlike other upwing flies. Its distribution is patchy and uncertain. The plan is to insert new examples of the nymph, the dun in both sexes, and the spinner in both sexes.

5) The Small Spurwing. *Centroptilum luteolum.*
Less rare, but hard to distinguish on the water from the generality of pale olives. Therefore, actually quite easy to imitate. The plan is to insert new examples of the nymph, the dun in both sexes, and the spinner in both sexes.

6) The Small Dark Olive. *Baetis scambus.*
Common in late Summer, widely distributed, and somewhat frustrating because it is so small – and not always dark. The plan is to insert new examples of the nymph, the dun in both sexes, and the spinner in both sexes.

7) The Pale Evening Dun. *Procloeon bifidum.*
Fairly patchy in distribution across the country although it used to be much more common, it's having just two wings makes it unmistakable in the hand or in the net, but in practical terms it is similar to the generality of pale olives and equally easy to imitate.

It does tend to hatch in the late afternoon or evening. The plan is to insert new examples of the nymph, the dun in both sexes, and the spinner in both sexes.

8) The Late, Summer, or False March Brown. *Ecdyonurus venosus.*
The nymph crawls out to hatch, and does not hatch at the surface, so the newly hatched dun is not important to the fly fisherman. The spinner is however, and so is the nymph. The plan is to insert new examples of the nymph, and the spinner in both sexes.

9) The Brook Dun. *Ecdyonurus torrentis.*
This large and impressive fly tends only to hatch in ones and twos and although trout will take it, they seldom selectively target it. Important on rain fed rivers all over the country. The plan is to insert new examples of the nymph, the dun in both sexes, and the spinner in both sexes.

10) The Autumn Dun. *Ecdyonurus dispar.*
The nymphs of this species also crawl out to hatch, limiting the usefulness of dun imitations – but the spinner (The Great Red Spinner) can be really quite useful, as can the nymph. The plan is to insert new examples of the nymph, and the spinner in both sexes.

11) The Turkey Brown. *Paraleptophlebia submarginata.*
This fairly large brown fly is fairly common although seldom present in large numbers such as to give rise to big hatches. However on rain fed rivers it can be extremely important as an imitative target, and there are signs of its increasing in abundance in the North. The plan is to insert new examples of the nymph, and of the dun in both sexes.

12) The Iron Blue. *Nigrabaetis niger.*
This is the rarer southern species which is really only an imitation target on the southern chalkstreams. Its colouration is different being more olivey and less purple, but a good imitation tied small and dark will do for either species. Both like to hatch in the rain. We have a full

set of examples of the more common one, *Alainites/Baetis muticus*. The plan is to insert new examples of the nymph, the dun in both sexes, and the spinner in both sexes of *Nigrabaetis*.

13) The Yellow May Dun. *Heptagenia sulphurea*.
This startlingly beautiful fly is more abundant and quite widespread away from the southern chalkstreams, and is a worthwhile imitative target on rain fed rivers elsewhere in the country. Although it is a trickle emerger rather than a hatch emerger, it is well taken by trout where it occurs in any numbers. The plan is to insert new examples of the male dun and the female spinner.

Peter Barnard's photo of Mosely's tying of the Yellow Sally (*Isoperla grammatica*) donated by PB to the club following rescue from the BNHM recycling bin

Also available from Coch-y-Bonddu Books

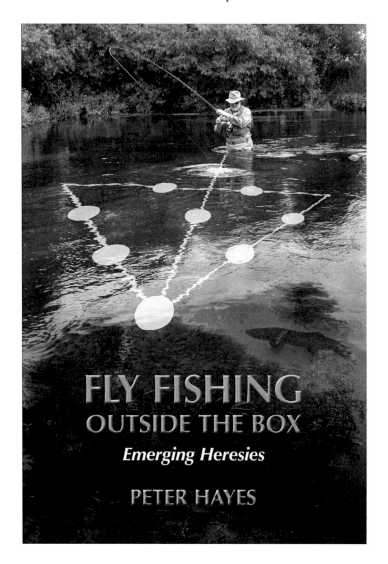